LOSS
of the
GROUND-NOTE

women writing about the loss of their mothers

Edited by Helen Vozenilek

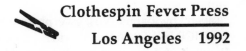

Clothespin Fever Press

Los Angeles   1992

082492

"Slipping into Stone"from LEAK IN THE HEART by Faye
Moskowitz. Copyright © 1985 by Faye Moskowitz. Reprinted by
permission of David R. Godine, Publisher.
"Forgotten Sorrow" by Susan Christian appeared as "Family Si-
lence Shrouds a Mother's Life." Copyright, © 1989, Los Angeles
Times. Reprinted by permission.
"Mother" from LATER THE SAME DAY by Grace Paley. Copy-
right © 1985 by Grace Paley. Reprinted by permission of Farrar,
Straus & Giroux, Inc.
"Why Is the Moon Cracked?" by Joan Campbell. Copyright ©1985
by Joan Campbell. First published in *Crosscurrents, a quarterly*. Re-
printed by permission of Joan Campbell.
The lines from "Transcendental Etude" are reprinted from THE
DREAM OF A COMMON LANGUAGE, Poems 1974-1977, by
Adrienne Rich, by permission of the author and W.W. Norton &
Company, Inc. Copyright © 1978 by W.W. Norton & Company, Inc.
"An Account" by Judith McCombs. Copyright © 1989 *Kansas Quar-
terly.* Reprinted by permission of *Kansas Quarterly.*
"On Passing" by Laura Munter-Orabono © 1990 from MAKING
FACE, MAKING SOUL/HACIENDO CARAS edited by Gloria
Anzaldua © 1990. Reprinted by permission of Aunt Lute Books
(415) 558-8116.
"The Pink Room" by Carolyn Weathers. Copyright © February
1992 by *Lone Star Literary Quarterly.* Reprinted by permission of the
author.
"Taken" by Joanna Woś, excerpt from SANAPIA: COMANCHE
MEDICINE WOMAN by David E. Jones, Copyright © 1972 by Holt,
Rinehart and Winston, Inc. Reprinted by permission of the pub-
lisher.
"For My Mother, Geneva" by Marilyn Carmen appeared as
"Momma's Girl" in *New Directions for Women.* Copyright © Febru-
ary 1991. Reprinted by permission of the author.

Acknowledgements

An anthology, perhaps more than any other publication, owes its existence to a number of people. So, first and foremost, I am grateful to all the women whose stories are contained within. And to the hundreds of other women who through letters, conversation and writings have shared their experiences of motherloss with me.

My thanks go also to:

Irene Zahava for the initial encouragement to do this book.
Carolyn Weathers and Jenny Wrenn, my publishers, for believing in *Loss of the Ground-Note* and seeing it to fruition, creating a trusting and productive relationship along the way.
Cheryle Holzaepfel and Sherry Clancy for help in reading manuscripts.
Robin Berman for her perceptive readings and exquisite sense of style and tone (most nearly matching my own!).
Molly Martin for her groundedness and no-nonsense approach to matters that didn't need futzing with, her craft and counsel, and for her shared club membership.
Risa Taylor for her encouragement to dig deeper and look harder, her intuition and insight, and for always believing this would be a great book. And always telling me so.
And to my father and the Smrčkas (Jiři, Zusana and Honsa) for my sense of roots.

in memory of my mother

September 4, 1921 – September 11, 1986

At most we're allowed a few months
of simply listening to the simple line
of a woman's voice singing a child
against her heart. Everything else is too soon,
too sudden, the wrenching-apart, that woman's heartbeat
heard ever after from a distance,
the loss of that ground-note echoing
whenever we are happy, or in despair.

– Adrienne Rich, *Transcendental Etude*

TABLE OF CONTENTS

Introduction   Helen Vozenilek/7

I. PARTING

II. WITHOUT A GOODBYE

III. VISITATIONS

IV. INHERITANCE

••••

———————— **INTRODUCTION** ————————

Helen Vozenilek

We move from a sense of need. Both others and our own. But what
we move toward is what moves us most.
– Susan Sherman, Ten Years Later

A friend once remarked that those of us without mothers
belong to a club of sorts. Not a club of our choosing, not a club
whose membership we covet or others strive to gain. There are
no secret handshakes or code words. Loss allows us admission.
The recognition of our loss links us as the most common de-
nominator. Recognition may come from simply seeing or reading or hearing a woman say two weeks, four months or sixty
years later, "I miss my mother."

As club members, we share certain rites, passages, experiences and understandings with each other. Some are the
objective factual sharings: What we do on Mother's Day, on her
birthday, on her death day? What were we doing when we
heard she died? What were our last words to her? What kind
of burial did she have? Then there are the less definable, the less
tangible outcroppings — our quicksands of grief, our reflecting
ponds of understanding, our lightning-flash illuminations of
our mothers/ourselves.

Though I speak of a club, my intent is not to exclude.
There are many others whose lives are affected by motherloss
and can benefit from this collection. These writings are for
friends, families and partners of women whose mothers have
died, to help share some of the feelings we are experiencing.
Those people who are in our lives when our mothers die, who
witness our sorrow and allow us the room to experience and
express our feelings, deserve volumes unto themselves. This
anthology is also for women who want to try to prepare themselves for the loss of their mothers.

The mother-daughter relationship is one of the most charged, complex and crucial relationships women will ever have. Some women may begin exploring this dynamic while their mother is alive. For others, a deeper search and scrutiny takes place after her death. This book explores what happens to the mother-daughter bond when it is severed through the mother's death.

I felt desolate, abandoned and intensely alone when my mother died. At twenty-eight, I was old enough to understand on a rational level that I was not the first person to have ever lost her mother. I knew other women who had lost theirs, had heard stories, read accounts, seen movies. But on a gut level I knew no one had ever experienced the pain and loss I was feeling. My grief felt huge and unassailable. This sense of our loss as unique and universal, separate and similar is one of the layers giving texture to this collection.

Motherless women all have stories about our mothers' deaths. Perhaps we've shared them with others — refrains, choruses or whole stanzas. Or perhaps we have held them close — with their joy and pain — in our hearts, and are only tentatively beginning to give them voice. Writing is but one medium through which women explore and share the experience of being motherless. Art, dance, song, ritual, storytelling are some of the other channels women use. More and more I notice these homages around me that women create for their mothers.

It has been tempting to generalize about the experiences of women losing their mothers, to sketch a pathway that clearly identifies signs and markers women will encounter. To say, "You will feel this way at first, a month later you will experience this, and six years later you can expect to feel this." I myself have often longed for some structure and theory that would compartmentalize and chart my pain. But, there is no single story or timetable or passageway through the sorrow. Some stories in this collection parallel my own, while others only occasionally intersect and overlap. The fact of our loss binds us together. The fact of our being motherless. Motherlessness is the common chord echoing in our lives and the common chord resonating in this anthology.

When I began this project, I wanted this book to be

everything to every woman who ever lost her mother. I wanted it to reflect every sentiment and emotion we have, to capture the pathos and foreverness of our loss, and to somehow fill that huge gaping hole. The impossibility of such a task soon became clear to me. These writings are but a prelude to the greater requiem of loss for our mothers.

The stories in this collection are divided into four sections. The opening section, *Parting*, moves from stories of daughters confronting their mothers' illness to death rituals. A daughter's parting extends from taking her mother on one last trip to the sea, to another watching the coffin lowered into the ground. Women's participation in these deathscapes ranges from eating breakfast with a mother unable to sit upright to another's curling her mother's hair in the funeral home.

The largest number of manuscripts I received were set against the backdrop of a mother's sickness or her funeral or burial arrangements. These settings —the hospital, the doctor's office, the graveyard, the funeral home — are the props around which we relive our mother's death. The tone of the mother's voice, the precise look of her body, the interactions and interplay during the mother's death passage remain indelibly marked in our memories.

For another group of women, there is neither space or permission for the parting ceremonies. In the second section, *Without a Goodbye*, women who are young when their mothers die or whose mothers die suddenly, tell of their loss. In this section, five women write of being denied information about their mother's life and death because of their youth. They write of a conspiracy of silence by family and friends whose intent was to spare the child pain. Years later, these women are still working to reclaim their grief.

Women whose mothers die unexpectedly must also learn to reclaim their grief. For the writer whose mother died "publicly" in a ship fire and another who received a note in the mail that her mother died, there was no time for closure. For these women, the suddenness of the event led to denial and a postponement of pain. They must work to create their own rituals of goodbye.

Mothers continue to appear long after they are physically

gone. In the third section, *Visitations*, women share images and memories of their mothers that follow them. A daughter senses her mother behind her in the cafeteria line, while another woman can't stop thinking about her mother's brain. Searching for her mother's gravesite unleashes a flood of memories for one writer, another converts a spare room in her house into a memorial to her mother. These stories show that through physical objects, gestures, phrases or sentience, mothers never really go away.

The final section, *Inheritance*, finds women looking back through their mothers' lives and forward through their own lives. The daughter's legacy is rich and many-layered. Women write of the fear and the joy of seeing parts of their mothers in themselves. For them it is a time to cast off and a time to inherit, a time for making breaks and a time for making amends. One writer compares the loss of her mother to the loss of a limb, another vows to be the tree her mother grew. One woman writes of the relationship with her mother as an "unfinished story," while others tell of the gifts they have inherited from their mothers. The process of continual search and resolution echoes through these stories.

Throughout the course of this book, I was continually humbled by the trust and openness with which women shared their stories. Some nights after reading submissions I would go to bed crying and awake red-eyed and hungover by loss. Other times I simply could not bear to read one more dead mother story. As a writer, I was amazed by the courage, honesty and insight with which women wrote of their mothers and themselves. As an editor, I was constantly dogged by the knowledge that I could only use a small number of the manuscripts I received.

Although not every woman's contribution could be included, each story has helped form, guide and steady the course of this anthology. It is to these contributors and to all motherless women who stand poised on a free-fall so piercing and so excruciatingly solitary that this book is dedicated.

PARTING

TWO STORIES

Judith Wolinsky Steinbergh
from stories told to her by Prilly Sanville

Bathing

It was before we took my mother to the sea but after we brought her home from New England Medical Center. Our day nurse Roberta, a Vermont native, hearty and affectionate, came days, and Angie came nights. Sundays, we were on our own. My brother, Andrew, came twice from Nebraska. Bess, my sister, covered when she could. But usually I drove up from Boston after work on Fridays and tried to get back to town Sunday nights.

At first I was pulled by the rituals of my weekend life, dinner out with a friend, a play or movie one night. I might rummage through the watercolors and drive up to Gloucester. I was resentful that I had to leave these comforts behind, the peace and companionship that allowed me to absorb the chaos of the work week with humor. I also wanted to be with my mother, to bring some comfort to her during her deteriorating health, maybe even repair some of our past differences. After several of these weekend trips, I began to look forward to leaving the city, to being embraced by the gentle Vermont hills. I would stop at the diner north of Concord on Route 89, then head for Winslow State Park and Sunapee, traveling forward and back at the same time.

Eventually, I began to lose touch. The hospital, its waiting rooms, corridors, coffee shop, its intensive care unit and rooms with cream colored textured wallpaper, the lawn in front with two redwood benches, and the woods behind, these things became my world. Nurses, doctors were my familiar faces. We grew solicitous in an odd way, seeking out things we had in common, hobbies, vacation spots, books and movies we loved.

When I brought my mother home, her room with the shades drawn was too confining for me. Each day, I walked past the old farms and newer clapboard houses, the blue trailer with the horse corral, and crossed Route 5 to the Rogers's meadow, smaller now since Mrs. Rogers sold off some of the acres, but still bordered by the windrow of poplars, and now, in late May, a snowdrift of daisies and buttercups. I stared at their lovely sagging red house and imagined spending the rest of my life here, tending to my mother and my garden, observing the wildlife and painting a little, maybe watercolor cards that would be sold in the college bookstores to campus visitors.

What I mean to say is that it's surprisingly easy to pull yourself away from your essential life, or to reconsider what is of value. And the work that has absorbed you, made you livid or given you extreme pleasure drifts away, becomes vague and irrelevant.

During the weekdays, in Boston, I read all of Kübler-Ross. I could reel off the five stages of dying, and I was determined to follow my mother's progress through these stages and help her in any way I could. My mother had passed through denial and was into anger. If I were dying I'd be pissed too. I wanted to say, "This must be difficult, you must feel angry," but I felt like a fool. She might look at me as if I'd lost my mind. I was busy being positive and imaging the healing process. For her, anger lasted a very long time. She may have never progressed to any other attitude, but one Friday night I arrived tired. My mother was as bitchy as ever, complaining about Roberta, Roberta who loved her like a sister.

I had thought about nothing else all week. "Ma," I said. "You can be angry for the next few months and keep us away from you. You can refuse our need to comfort you and be alone in this illness or you can let us love you. You aren't getting better. You decide." I straightened her sheets, carried her to the bathroom, changed her nightgown, and went to bed.

Somehow that propelled her into something new or freed her from years of resentment. "Come rub my back," she asked me Saturday morning. "Bring violets closer to me. Roberta brought them yesterday." And on Sunday, "Call Andrew now and let me hear his voice." "Send a birthday card to Bess's twins. I don't want them to think their grandma forgot them."

We ate some consomme together at lunch. A woodthrush sang through the woods and we were silent together, letting it make shining concentric circles in the air. "Sweetie," she said, reaching out feebly and touching my hair, "I like the way you're getting gray, in those lovely streaks."

She ate almost nothing now. A few ice chips, a little broth or pudding. Sometimes when I entered her room, she had almost no mass under the thin blanket. Then I wanted to remember her fighting. Today she asked me if she could take a bath. I called Roberta. She said that in all her years of nursing, no one in this late stage had taken anything more than a sponge bath. I could see my mother on the bed, silently muttering the word "bath." I offered once more, very nonchalantly, "My mother would really like to take a bath. How should I do it?"

"I'll be there in ten minutes." Roberta said, "Start the water and run it tepid." Roberta strode in. She soaked a blanket in the tub and spread it out on the bottom to protect my mother's bruised skin from the hard enamel. She propped two pillows against one end of the tub. She nodded. I lifted my mother from the high bed. She was so light, I thought she might float in the water like a bar of soap. I sat on the toilet and drew off her robe. Roberta untied her hospital gown. My mother barely had a body. It was scarred where they had tried to remove the cancer several times. She could no longer bother with modesty or pride. She shivered. It was very warm in the bathroom and humid from the running water. I let Roberta place her in the tub. Even a child could step in, but my mother was too weak to raise her legs. She looked disoriented for a minute, as if the feel of water all around her brought up a memory so vivid, it gave her some old strength or pleasure. She leaned back against the pillows, her hair damp and curled at the ends. She dipped her hands in the clear warm water and raised them up a little, letting the water drip through her fingers. She smiled. She did this again and turned her hands down to pat and splash softly like some thin old bird and then, almost imperceptibly, she began to sing. I was already on my knees sponging water over her legs, but I had to lean in to hear her. Roberta was changing the sheets. I hummed a little too, although it wasn't clear what melody my mother was singing. She dipped her hands in again and let the water make circles on the surface. "This is the happiest day of my life," my mother said, letting her fingers form a wake in the bath.

[15]

Her body rose in the water, let go a bit. I leaned back, trying to see her better. She had a beauty, not womanly, something else. I thought of a waterlily bloom, connected by an invisible stem to a dark place, its white blossom rising up, up, opening to the light.

Traveling

She wants to go to the sea. Outside the window, the bare trees redden on the Vermont hills. And in the hazy valleys, willows begin to yellow. She is a leaf herself. When I lift her from the high white bed, she is almost weightless. Sometimes I go into the hall to catch my breath, to try to absorb that I am the daughter of this woman who is partially light.

I ask the day nurse what she thinks about making a journey to the coast with my mother.

"It will be very hard on her," Roberta says. I make no response. Roberta is massaging my mother's shoulder, her thin blue arm. "She grew up by the sea, didn't she?" I nod. "Was it near Bath?"

"Yes, did she tell you that? In Georgetown, actually. My grandparents moved there from the city just after the war. We often went back there when we were young. There's a beautiful beach nearby, at the state park."

"If she really wants to go and you're willing to risk it, you ought to give it a try."

Doctor Reed stops by. The i.v., the monitors will be problems. Doctor Lynch returns my call. Pneumonia is a danger. The blockages might grow worse. It depends what we want for her. What *we* want for her?

I sit by the bed of my mother whose skin is already transparent. Her delicate bones pull tight the freckled flesh of her cheeks.

"Is this what you really want to do?"

She nods. Barely.

Do you know what might happen? But no more words come out and inside, I say, yes, I do.

She says in a voice so thin, it might be air in aspen trees, "It will be fine. I want to go to the sea. I want to touch the water." This tires her and she closes her eyes.

I call my sister Bess and my brother Andrew. They can be here tomorrow. We will go on Tuesday. I call friends in Boston. They'll meet us at Plum Island, the barrier sand bar that protects Newburyport. We will have to carry her across the beach.

Andrew was here two weeks before. Now the body of our mother is so much less than it was, to carry her seems like nothing. We can make a sensible plan, but if her life can't complete this journey, how will we respond?

Bess comes in that morning. It is a soft spring day. A day when roses begin in Boston, but here it is still rhododendrons, azaleas, tulips. Roberta slips a flannel bathrobe around my mother's shoulders. The slippers hang off of her frail feet. Roberta turns her onto one side and spreads a blanket, then a sheet beside her. From the side, there is no sign that my mother is breathing. Her white hair is matted against one cheek and flattened to the back of her head, which also seems flatter than before. I remember her with wings for hair. The gray-white waves brushed out like gulls.

What on earth are we thinking of. Andrew stands half facing out to the hallway. Bess bends down and gently combs my mother's hair. Roberta kisses her on the forehead. She whispers that she will see her tomorrow. Say hello to the ocean for her. Bring her a shell.

Soon I will be a motherless child. The song pours into my head like amber molasses, like the wailing, healing blues.

I touch Andrew's shoulder. He looks around puzzled as if he'd forgotten our plan. We turn my mother onto the blanket and sheet and wrap them around her. My own infant was delivered to me this way, wrapped in pink lace and blankets. I wondered which end was her head.

Andrew kneels down by the side of her bed. He bends over and his forehead touches where her thigh would be under the white blanket. He stays that way for what seems like a very long time, rocking slightly. Then he straightens up. He puts his arms under the blanket and stands up. She is small and limp like someone who has already died, or is just born. One blue terry slipper falls off. Bess picks it up. My mother's head presses into Andrew's shoulder, her white hair disappears in his white cotton shirt. She smiles faintly. She is leaving home. She is leaving for the sea she loves, grit and salt, pebble clack and tides, sea froth and kelp hold, mussel shell and sea slide, words that endure.

Bess drives. Andrew stares at a map he doesn't need to use. In the back seat, I hold my mother. I cradle the life in her. I breathe for her. I breathe until the salt comes in and I know we will arrive. Then my mother says, thank you, soundlessly, the way water seeps into and darkens sand.

Author's note: These stories are dedicated with love and respect to Cynthia Sanville —

WHY IS THE MOON CRACKED?

Joan Campbell

I am escaping from somewhere along with a lot of people I don't know. All of us are crawling on the edge of something dragging our gear in large laundry sacks behind us, and along the way I keep finding coins. I keep stuffing the coins into my pockets. I figure I might need them. Sometimes I have to brush the ground to uncover them so I know we are crawling on dirt. But we are on the edge of something. A cliff or maybe a river bank.

Ahead of me is an old woman who has apparently made the trip before. She has a long gray braid and a guidebook that looks outdated, like it was written in the fifties. I keep asking if she is sure this is the way — the path has steadily become more slanted, as if we were crawling along a roof line and at any moment could go tumbling off — but she says yes, she is sure. This is the way.

Suddenly the path ends. It is dark, the quarters are cramped, and we are still balancing on the edge. There are beams along a type of ceiling which we must brace ourselves against to keep from sliding off. We are at such a perilous angle!

Finally the old woman decides that we must go around the obstruction and swing down to the next level. Each of us is to rely on the person behind us for help. I grab her forearm and she grabs mine, but as she swings around and down, out of view, I awake to the sound of feet scrambling on loose shale, her hand quietly slipping from mine.

Breakfast is hurried as usual. Toast and eggs for Carl, lightly browned and over easy, and pancakes for the children in the shapes of animals. I make no mention of the dream. I have been having lots of dreams lately.

"What's this?" Joey asks.

I hand him the syrup and tell him it's a giraffe. Can't he tell by the long neck?

"It looks like a weird monster," he says.

"Stupid dope," says Lisa. Lisa is three years older and therefore superior.

"Lisa," says Carl.

Normally I would be having either toast or cereal, but I'm not feeling hungry. Today I will go again to the hospital. I will take the kids to the sitter and kiss Carl off to work and I will pick up my father who still pretends nothing is wrong. Everything is fine. They are doing all they can for her.

"Everything is just fine, kiddo," he says. But, of course, it's a lie.

Today we find a strange machine outside her room. She's still in Intensive Care, but I keep thinking of it as her room because she's been here so long. Two weeks, anyway. Or has it been three?

The machine is a respiration unit. It has an oxygen blender made in Palm Springs and it comes just up to my chest. It's on wheels, of course — everything here of importance is — so they can rush it from room to room, floor to floor, in and out of elevators, to give a dose of life to the dying, a quick breath of hope to the slow hopeless. The model number, I notice, is an MA-1.

The door blooms open and a nurse comes out who is young, my age. She tells us we can go in now. In a slow but dignified shuffle my father moves ahead, his cane tapping an even path on the floor.

"We were just changing the dressing," she says. "She's doing pretty well, considering."

I nod, but already she belongs to someone else. She belongs to the old man now with the even older cough that might be pneumonia, cancer, emphysema. Whatever it is, no one speaks of it. Words might transmit infections here that cannot be cured.

Aside from the old man and my mother, there are two others: a woman with her forehead wrapped in bandages, and a small boy about Joey's age with his leg in traction. Is she the boy's mother? Were they in an accident? Will they be all right? The room is stale with the smell of unanswered questions.

My mother looks about the same. Her forehead is pale and smooth like a child's, a network of veins running beneath the skin like rivers of spilled ink. She's hooked up to a machine that broadcasts her pulse in bright red digits, and she still has a quarter-sized disk at the base of her neck. Her pulse this morning fluctuates between eighty and eighty-five.

"Hello, bebbe!"

Good cheer and a stiff upper lip are my father's answers for everything, his means of coping. He stoops to brush his lips against her dry forehead, and if he looks at her throat it is only fleetingly, the way one slides off the face of truth, or the bereaved.

She can't answer, of course: she has a hole in her throat. She has a hole with a stainless steel tube running down it, and when she moves her mouth it's like watching an old silent movie. Still, in the midst of all this silence, there is a profound need for words, words that will tie up the empty spaces to recreate something smooth and seamless.

I hand her a folded piece of paper. "From Lisa," I explain. "It's supposed to be you in the hospital, but I'm afraid she sort of stuck you on a fence."

My mother grins, lost for the moment in the bright streaks of crayon.

"They really do miss you," I say.

She nods. She misses them, too.

"I brought your slippers," my father says. "Also the crossword puzzle."

He tosses a small sack to the foot of her bed, and the newspaper onto her table, but my mother stares at him as if he were half crazy. Slippers? When would she be needing those? What could he be thinking, this man with whom she has shared children, a life?

No time for questions now, though. She has bent double, powerless and frail, her face twisting as the fiery cough rises. Her pulse rate, I notice, leaps to an alarming 135.

The nurse hurries over to tell us we must go now. "Please," she says.

As if we caused it. As if we caused the pain.

It started as a small lump. Something in a child's pocket. A mystery. Then it got bigger. "Maybe you should get that checked," we said. But, of course, it was nothing. A bruise, a swollen gland. The next thing we know, she's in the hospital. Some kind of tumor, they said, but they had to run tests. CAT scan. Barium X ray. Biopsy. They wanted to get going on it pretty fast. The tumor was pressing on her windpipe, interfering with her breathing.

The tests were the worst part. For one she had to put her tongue in a vice while they sprayed stuff in her mouth that made her gag. "If I can get through that," she said, "I can get through anything."

Which was good because the biopsy ended up backfiring. All that poking around apparently caused the tumor to swell until it closed off her windpipe entirely. That's when they had to do the tracheotomy, and we almost lost her.

When she awoke, with the fire in her throat, she said she almost wished we had. Lost her, I mean.

Yet my father keeps insisting there's nothing to worry about. Today as I drive him back home, he reminds me of all the other things she's been through: two C-sections, appendectomy, double mastectomy, duodenal tumor. What I can't figure out is if he really believes she'll be okay or if it's just wishful thinking. Does he know something I don't know?

I know we need to talk. We need to air the sheets, open all the rooms and tame this dark beast, but my feelings have amassed in a large clot at the back of my throat which refuses to budge.

When I open my mouth, what comes out is simply, "Why don't you come have supper with us tonight?"

His hands grip the top of his cane like talons. "What do you mean, Selina? I've got leftover chicken. I'm fine," he says. "No sense worrying about me."

When Carl gets home from work he asks, "How'd it go?"

"The same," I say.

We have just rented an old two-story house with turrets and lots of nooks and crannies. Somewhere in the dream comes the realization that this house is significant. My mother's oldest brother, dead now, once lived here along with Carl, some old school friends, my brother-in-law. I have visited all of them here before. Someone dies in the dream. A roommate?

Carl and I go to visit friends. When we enter their living room we find two men who tell me I should put on my glasses. But I don't know these men, so how do they know I wear glasses? Carl makes himself comfortable and begins to read, so I go into the kitchen only to find my mother. What is she doing here? I start to tell her about the remarkable house we've found and all of its coincidences, but she keeps interrupting to ask why we moved. She doesn't understand why we didn't tell her first. I get angry at her for not understanding and we begin to fight.

The end of the dream appears as the end of a story which relates in printed type all that has gone on before.

(Something deep in the conscious mind stirs. Why has the dream switched genres? Am I not strong enough to withstand the dream's reality?)

In the margin of the story are some digits I can't decipher. When I hold them up to the mirror, though, it all comes clear. The digits say SENTENCED TO DEATH. But who is to die? Me? My mother?

When I awake, damp and trembling, Carl is rocking me back and forth, saying, "It's okay, Selina. It's okay."

But it's not okay, and maybe that's what bothers me. Everyone is pretending that everything's okay when, in fact, things are lousy. The children have been keeping their rooms immaculate. Twice I have overheard Carl telling them to be on their best behavior. Once a week, for the past month, Carl has brought flowers home after work. Somehow, instead of comforting me, these actions just seem to have made things worse. It's as if my family had placed me on a riverboat. I am destined to make a long voyage alone, while the members of my family wave me on from shore. What I really want is for them to let me come home. I want to tell them, she isn't dead yet.

"It'll all work out, kiddo," my father says.

I fight to keep from jerking the steering wheel. Today he looks especially dapper. Though there is a harsh, angular quality to his face, he looks young in his best suit and yellow string tie — certainly nowhere near seventy — and as we wait for the elevator I notice he's polished his cane. The tip of it shines like a child's faith, like an old man's touch of hope, and something about this small careful act makes me suddenly ashamed. I feel that I've been too hard on him. I feel that I've been too hard on everyone, including myself.

My mother looks better today. There's a strange light that

shines in her eyes and when my father bends to kiss her, this light seems to flare.

She takes my hand, then just as quickly releases it to grope for something under the sheet. Out comes a piece of cardboard with a shiny grey square on it. Then, a pencil-shaped, pointed stick attached to it with a string. Slowly, painstakingly, she begins to write on the grey square: *Look what they gave me!* She holds it up so we both can see, and I realize that it's the same thing Carl and I gave as a toy, last Christmas, to Joey. It has Mickey and Minnie Mouse dancing across the top of it, and when you write on it, you can lift a sheet of clear plastic and everything is erased. Joey thinks it's magic, just as my mother does.

Look! she writes, eagerly touching my arm. She fumbles for the edge of the plastic, and with one quick flick of the page, all is gone, as if the words simply never existed.

While she busies herself writing something else, I look around and notice for the first time that the small boy is gone. *Gone.* His mother — or at least the woman I've imagined to be his mother — is sleeping soundly, but I can see through all the bandages the dark bruises of her eyes.

Once more my own mother tugs at me. I read what she has written: *Changed dressing myself today.*

She tilts her head back so we can see and, sure enough, just beneath the disk at the base of her throat is a fresh square of gauze. It has only a small trace of blood on the edge of it, so I can tell that it's been changed recently.

"That's great," I say weakly. My father agrees, and though I feel slightly dizzy, I try to keep reading as casually as if I were scanning a grocery list. *Tomorrow I suction,* it says. *First lesson today.* She points to the machine, now by her bed, the one with the Palm Springs oxygen blender, but the nurse is giving us the eye. My mother holds up her arm, then hastily scribbles one more note: *Give Joey and Lisa big hug from Grandma.*

Outside, the nurse says the doctor would like to see us. She assures us that it's just routine. I ask her then about the boy. Did he —?

"It happened so fast," she says, shaking her head. The nausea rises, an uninvited shadow. My father makes a clicking sound with his tongue. Too bad. A terrible thing. I need desperately to ask if that woman in there is his mother, but I also need desperately not to know.

When the nurse goes back in, I catch sight of the boy's bed, empty now, with fresh, white, flawless sheets.

It's almost as if he's been erased. It's almost as if he never existed.

The doctor is cool, practical. "We still can't be sure, he says. "It *is* malignant but we need to run more tests, find out just what kind of cancer it is."

My father watches him with the unquestioning trust one reserves for idols. To my father, this man can do no wrong. This man has saved his wife's life. He must not cross this man or offend him in any way.

"Do whatever you have to do," he says quietly. "I just want Rosie to come home."

I, on the other hand, am tired of having to read between the lines. And though I don't want to just blurt it out, I can't really think of a better way to ask it, a kinder way to put the question. I give my father an apologetic look, then turn back to the doctor. "How long does she have?"

Moments. Years.

"There's no way of knowing," he says finally. "Could be weeks, could be . . . ."

"But surely you can give us *some* idea."

My father stands, taking my arm. "Come, Selina. The doctor is a busy man."

I have moved with my father to a large two-storied Victorian house. It's a nice house, run-down but cozy. I keep thinking that when my father dies how will I ever take care of it all? The heaviness of the responsibility makes me decide that I really don't like it here after all. The next thing I know, I'm walking along a frontage road headed for home . . . .

"Mama?"

Somewhere a child is crying.

"Mommie?"

Dimly, sluggishly, I rise from the cellar of sleep, only to find my son Joey lying on top of me. Tiny tears are falling down his face like streaks of rain.

"What's wrong, Joey?   Did you have a bad dream? "

Stubbornly he clings to me, his hot face pressed against my chest. "A might-mare," he says.

"Oh, honey, I'm sorry. Mommie was having a nightmare, too."

For some reason this seems to improve his spirits. He lifts his sleepy head and says, "You were? Honest?"

"What is it?" Carl says, rolling over.

I tell him it's nothing. I tell him it's just Joey and I'll see if I can take care of it. I get up from the bed, Joey's arms like a yoke around my neck, and together we head for the rocking chair by the window. We sit and we rock, Joey's small head bobbing against my chest, and for a time we're both silent — lulled by the view of all the houses framed in the grey sky, and in the distance, the fine web of jewels spun by the city.

In time, Joey squirms, turning around to look at me.

"Do you really have might-mares?" he asks. "Honest to goodness? With monsters and everything?"

"Oh, Joey," I say. "There are no monsters."

I realize then that I'm taking the same tack that my father has taken with me: I'm trying to protect him. I know without a doubt that there are all kinds of monsters, and sooner or later they're coming down the road for us all. I just hadn't wanted Joey to know about them yet. And yet . . . .

He studies me carefully. I can tell he's not about to let this one slide. But just as I'm about to explain that yes, there are monsters, little tiny unseeable monsters and great big unknowable monsters, he turns back to the window and says, "Why is the moon cracked?"

At first, I don't understand what he's talking about. Then he points to the moon, off to our left, folded in half like a big paper plate, and I get a strange feeling that he's pointing the way to a whole new landscape — which, of course, he is.

Yet how do I explain about spheres whirling through space, spheres that cast shadows over other spheres until soon, overshadowed, there seems to be nothing left? However I approach it, I know it's a rare opportunity. Here is my chance to do for my son what I have wished, for so long, my father would do for me.

"The moon is cracked," I say, taking a deep, uneven breath, "because it's trying to say goodbye to the sun."

Joey's eyes grow wide with astonishment. It's as if he were trying to make sense of a puzzle designed for an older child.

"But that's silly," he says finally. "The sun comes up every morning."

"That's right," I say, "but the moon sometimes forgets that. Sometimes the moon gets in places where it doesn't remember."

He lets his head fall back to my chest, as if to let this new knowledge sink in. He's getting more than he bargained for, and I'm not sure how much he can absorb, how much any of us can absorb. But I do know he will try very hard to understand.

When he speaks, his voice is so low I can barely hear him.

"Is that what you've been doing?" he asks, staring into the dark.

"What, Joey?"

Again, he is not sure. He seems to sense that he's standing on shaky ground and that in order to grasp what I'm saying he must make a tremendous leap.

"With Grandma," he says finally.

For moments, years, we spin through a web of stillness, a space of terrible silence, until sheepishly he turns to me ready, if need be, to dive behind his hands. This is the edge I have come to in my dreams. This is the place where if I'm not careful we both could fall.

I wait for the clot to form at the back of my throat. I wait for the words to stop, for the rocking to cease, but it's all out in the open now as the words emerge to lead us back from the edge.

"Yes, Joey," I say, nestling my face in the damp mystery of his hair. "I am learning, ever so slowly, how to say goodbye."

MY MOTHER'S HAIR

Judy A. Ashley

My father died when I was nine. My therapist said I can't remember because it was a shock and I blotted it out of my mind. My mother died last May. It's December now. This is my first Christmas without parents. A child of no one. Not a child really. I am thirty-five.

When my mother died I wanted to remember. I held her hand when she died. She stopped breathing just like in the movies. You know, they take a breath and then they don't. I never believed that was really the way people died, but that's how my mother did. Her hand grew cold immediately. I cried and kissed her forehead. Even the nurses cried. I shouldn't have been sad because she was seventy-two years old but she was my Mom and I knew I would miss her.

The next day I went to the funeral home and the undertaker brought me to the casket room to pick out a casket. All funeral homes have a room like this with all kinds of caskets. They have caskets with mahogany wood and real silk lining and "guaranteed not to leak" caskets. Every kind you can imagine except a pine box. I didn't care much about what kind of wood the casket was made of except I surely didn't want mahogany. Mom would have gone crazy if I paid five thousand dollars for a mahogany box that was going to rot and nobody would see anyway. All I was interested in was the color inside. I wanted it to be blue to match her eyes and so she would feel like she was in the sky.

I decided that I wanted to fix her hair. I talked to the funeral man and he said I shouldn't worry about it because he has someone who does that all the time. But, I said, how's this person going to know how my mother liked her hair fixed? I'm the one who fixed it for her ever since I was tall enough to reach her head.

I used to curl her hair every week. We always had a good

time. She would wash it and I would put on the rollers. My mother was old-fashioned. No blow dry, drip dry styles for her. When she curled her hair she did it with rollers and picks. She would hand me the rollers and picks, and I would put them in her hair. Sometimes I would give her a perm. That was fun except perms smell like rotten eggs and rubbing alcohol mixed together. Mom always said I did a great job even if I accidently left the perm solution on too long. It seemed natural to me that I should fix her hair one last time. The funeral man finally agreed.

I got to the funeral home bright and early the next morning. I had my curling iron, comb and rollers. The funeral man led me down long narrow stairs into a big room like the casket room. The floor was tiled. That was the first thing I noticed. Right away I figured it was because they spilled the embalming fluid. The room reminded me of an operating room. It was cold and empty with bright fluorescent lights glaring from a stained, faded ceiling. Mom was lying on a steel table with a white sheet over her. At first glance she didn't look much different. Her head was propped up on a wooden block and her hair was straight and stiff like an old straw broom.

The funeral man showed me the curling iron that the other woman used. It was an old-fashioned kind with a little oven and heavy iron rods. I told him I had my own curling iron. He said he would turn the other one on — just in case.

I surveyed the situation and wasn't sure where to start. I started to comb her hair but wasn't making much progress. The funeral man was hanging around and making me nervous. He probably thought I would collapse in tears or pass out. I finally told him he could leave because I had my work cut out for me. He said he would leave but he wouldn't go too far away — just in case.

After he left, I started talking to Mom. After all, we always talked when I did her hair. I didn't see anything wrong with it. I told her her hair was a mess. I told her she would die if she could see it. Then I started to laugh.

My curling iron wouldn't curl her hair after all. It wasn't hot enough. I guess the funeral man knew what he was talking about. I used the old-fashioned iron and burned her hair right away. I panicked and almost changed my mind. What if I

burned all the hair on her head? What would everyone think?
I told myself that if I burned it once more I would stop. Then I
apologized to Mom, cut off the burned piece, and continued
working.

I worked and talked. Sometimes I worried about the
funeral man catching me talking to a dead body. After awhile,
though, there was just me and Mom. I told her about my job and
things about the family. There were moments when I was sure
I heard her voice. The hours passed quickly. It was just like old
times.

VIOLET '86

Sapphire

The brown velvet doll has cowrie shells for eyes and lips and long braids of my own hair. She is the first doll I ever made. I call her Little Africa, L.A. for short. You won't take her. You are afraid someone in the hospital will steal my gift to you. Or that the hospital staff won't allow you to keep her.

I finger the necklace I've taken from your house. I admonish myself. You are not dead yet. Fingering the round purple beads, I think of your house full of purple towels, knickknacks, and yarn.

"Why purple Mommy?" I ask. "Why purple?"

"For love, passion." You say the doll is beautiful, adorable, but still you do not take her. I tell you I made her. I tell you I am not angry anymore.

You wave your hand at my need to say what you already know.

"I love you."

"I know. I love you, too."

I pick the doll up and make her dance, bouncing her up and down on your bed. I am singing and dancing as I make the doll dance. I hold her up. She says, *I love you*, with her cowrie shell mouth, her asymmetrical legs bouncing in the air.

"I love you, too," you answer.

I put the doll away and stand to leave. "I just came to say goodbye."

You are so sad, little and brown. "Don't say goodbye, just say 'so long.'"

The nurse beckons to me as I approach your door. She tells me you have pulled off your oxygen mask and have barricaded yourself in the bathroom to smoke a cigarette. You feel everyone is against you. I wonder if you are crazy or suffering from oxygen deprivation. Forewarned, I peek my head around the door. You turn to me like a little hurt bird. You are glad to see me. I am not part of the plot against you. The nurse and I exchange glances of relief.

Everyone is against you, except me and Dr. Staddon. Dr. Staddon has a program where you could die with some peace and dignity. Everyone else wants you to take the chemo. You can't breathe. One lung is collapsed. The pneumonia is a particularly virulent kind. The pneumonia compounds the leukemia, the leukemia the pneumonia. A catheter would be inserted into your aorta, the poison would be pumped into your body. It would immediately kill off the leukemia cells and you. *And you* is what they neglect to tell you. But you know. Deep inside you know.

The next day, I walk into your room. A monster is sitting on your bed. His face is covered with white gauze. He is dressed in thin sick-blue paper pants and coat. On his head is a shower cap, white plastic bags cover his shoes. He is coarse, red and ugly. He is rich. He is white. He is the surgeon come to get you to sign papers to pump poison into your aorta. I am poor. I am black. I am a woman.

I run to you. The demon refuses to move. His gloved hand moves to the papers, but my hand is upon them first.

"What are the possible dangers of this type of surgery?"

"Well, of course," he says as if he is addressing a mosquito, "infection, lung collapse — ."

"Lung collapse!"

"Well, the catheter could possibly puncture the lung when it is being inserted — ."

"Which lung?"

"*Which* lung?" he echoes.

"One lung is already collapsed as a result of the pneumonia."

"Oh, of course, then, we would, ahh, insert it over the other lung."

"Which is?"

"Well, I don't know all that — ."

"How will the operation itself affect her pneumonia since she already has trouble breathing?"

"I can't answer all that," he snaps, "I just put the catheter in. I'm the surgeon."

"He doesn't know if this will be in your best interest," I say slowly. "You don't have to do this. It's to his economic advantage to perform as many operations as possible. I don't think this is a good idea."

You pat my black hand. Already my veins protrude like yours. You hand the paper to the doctor and tell me, "You shouldn't have come. The doctors know, and your brother thinks this is best."

"When?" I ask, only now realizing that I'm too late. You have signed the papers.

"In a few days."

"*When?*"

"A week from now, Wednesday."

I look at you, broken, brown and dying. I try to tell myself that maybe, maybe you can stand the onslaught. Maybe you know something I don't. Maybe . . . a miracle.

Two days after the tube is inserted you are dead.

The business of death takes away feeling and gives detachment. Everywhere my hands perform a last prayer, folding, stacking, discarding, cleaning. Bag after bag of trash hauled in the heat, scrubbing a filthy toilet seat, scraping mold out of dishes, dusting, determining , separating, saving. What is to be saved after sixty-five years? What is trash and what is valuable? I take your sewing machine, the purple vases that graced your window, the sewing kit, Bible, watches, leather gloves, perfume, pictures and letters.

I clean and clean. Finally there is a four-foot stack in front of your dresser. Your sister can sort through these things. But I can't find the one picture I want most. And letters, I feel there were more.

The house is clean and orderly. No one will come in here thinking you were a crazy, dirty, old lady. Your bedside is neat and elegant. I leave incense burning in an iridescent mauve ashtray, one of the last things you made. It says "Violet '86" underneath. A radical departure in color and style from the work of twenty years ago that says "Lofton." I leave lavender towels hanging, the refrigerator clean, the plants watered. I draw the curtains. A candle burns. Aretha Franklin drifts poignant and haunting from an ancient record player, *"Hey, Baby, let's get away . . . someplace far . . . . "*

I've cleared all the tables that were stacked with magazines and dirty ashtrays. All over, you had crystal bowls filled with matches and candy. These are washed out and emptied. I stare at the bottle in my hand. "Pure pack solution 1% Gentian Violet (aqueous)." I fill the bowls with water, flick drops of the deep purple solution into the bowls. Slowly the deep dark drops expand turning the water into a wonderful clear purple color. The house is sweet-smelling and peaceful.

I turn off Aretha gently and stand looking over where you used to live. You wanted me to bring my friends, to meet them. I never did. Too much water under the bridge, I thought then, to play mother and daughter. But, I stand here now, dusty and tired in my daughter's duty. You are gone now, all possibilities closed like the coffin over your face. We have no tomorrows you and I, only a past and places in my dreams. I whisper hesitantly on my way out the door, "Come on back and see me if you can."

FLO'S FUNERAL

Molly Martin

Two days after his phone machine message brought the news of my mother's death, my father's voice had regained some life. "I've been thinking about the funeral and I have an idea," he said. "I'd like all the pallbearers to be women. Your mother would have wanted it, don't you think?"

The suggestion filled me with pride for my father and gratitude. I'd always assumed that his liberal or feminist ideas were a product of my mother's prompting. Could he have thought of this himself? Whatever the sources I was thrilled and said I wanted very much to be a pallbearer. Then I got on the phone to my brother, Don.

Don is my closest ally in the family. Not only are we both gay, but we also share a similar world view. Both critical of the status quo, we are our mother's children and identify with her much more than do our two younger brothers. As adults, we began addressing our mother as Flo — instead of Mom or Florence — because she felt more like our friend than our mother. Flo's funeral service was of great symbolic significance to us; we wanted her to be remembered for the things we truly loved about her. Our worst fear was that conservative religious relatives would take over and whitewash the service. So we began to conspire, and also to prepare for the possibility of disappointment.

My parents were Presbyterians though not particularly devout. I suspected both to be closet agnostics (my father once confessed to me that he believes we turn into stars when we die). The minister of their church had been called out of town, so my father had asked a preacher he'd met at an AA encounter group to give the service. Never having known my mother, the preacher called the family together to provide some substance for his remarks. My father, grandmother, three brothers, two sisters-in-law and I met him at the funeral home the day before the service.

Fat, rumpled and red-cheeked, the preacher arranged us in a circle and I wondered if this was how he ran the AA group. Would we be expected to introduce ourselves? "Hi. My name is Molly and I 'm motherless." Instead, he began to instruct us in a familiar country drawl. The service, he explained, would be brief. The family would sit behind a curtain in a private alcove and he would eulogize Florence in a short sermon. What would we like him to say? He folded his hands on his lap in studied calm. This was his work-a-day fare; he had prepared countless funeral services, counseled many bereaved families.

We looked at each other uncertainly. None of us knew how funerals are produced. We certainly hadn't expected participatory democracy.

"Tell me about Florence," intoned the preacher. "Was she a good mother?"

This was exactly what I'd feared. How could we move the topic beyond motherhood without sounding un-American?

Don, dark eyes focused intensely behind horn-rimmed glasses, gripped the arms of his chair and sat forward. "Yes, she was a good mother, but not in traditional ways. That's not mainly how we remember her. It was her politics. She hated war and imperialism."

I saw scowls forming on the others' faces and tried to signal my brother to curb his rhetoric.

"Flo was a true humanist," I amended. "She was personally grieved by people's suffering anywhere in the world." I paused. I wanted to satisfy everyone. "She was a good mother because she made us feel her involvement, she expected us to be aware of our world."

"I have a favorite passage from the Bible about motherhood. Shall I quote it?" asked the preacher.

Don and I exchanged a glance. We had hoped we could avoid patriarchal religion altogether. Across the circle, Flo's mother, Gerda, was nodding, visibly pleased at the Bible verse. The family matriarch at ninety-four, she commanded respect, and we understood the significance of this service for her. Till the day she died, Flo had been Gerda's closest friend and main family support. The two had talked on the phone at least daily and Flo had driven across town to visit several times a week. The church was the center of Gerda's life. We surrendered a point to her.

"Did Florence take part in civic affairs?" asked the preacher. His plump fingers glided across the page, and I imagined him writing "civic affairs" in big loopy script.

"Florence was a kind of a crusader," my father said. "She was active in several organizations. We made up a list for the obituary — Amnesty International, NOW, Yakima Living Historians, the Red Cross."

Don pushed his foot-long pigtail to the back of his head. "She was involved in the feminist, anti-war, prison and anti-nuclear movements," he added.

The preacher kept writing, so we kept talking, all the while suspecting our remarks were being edited for consumption by the silent majority.

"Florence served in the Red Cross for two years with the Third Division in Europe," said my father. "Make sure you say something about that."

"She was at the liberation of Dachau," added Don. "She only started to talk about it in the last few years. It was very traumatic for her, and she said it was one reason for her anti-war work."

I smiled to myself as I remembered marching with Flo in a spirited demonstration to the university president's house on one student-mother weekend while the other mothers were shopping and watching fashion shows. Her favorite chant was, "One, two, three, four, we don't want your fucking war!" because we could yell "fucking" at the top of our lungs. By that time, in efforts to defend me in brushes with university regulations, she had begun a regular correspondence with the president. He would see me on campus and embarrass me, the student radical, by asking about my mother.

"She was a writer," I said.

"Oh?" said the preacher, "What did she write?"

We hesitated. We wished Flo had written her autobiography, especially the stories she told about her years as a Red Cross "donut girl" in World War II, but we had found only a couple of short stories and some essays written for adult-ed classes. We all felt she had been brilliant. Her fondest wish as a girl was to go to college, but the Depression had made that impossible. Instead, when her father lost his job, she became the

[37]

family breadwinner at sixteen, working as a secretary.

"She wrote letters to the editor," I said. "She wrote to her Congress people." This sounded inadequate. I remembered a letter she'd sent me a carbon of a couple of years before. "Dear Mr. President," it began, and continued to detail the horrors of war, then proposed that the government spend money instead to work on peace. She'd called to ask what I thought.

"Wonderful!" I said. "Send it."

"I did," she said, "ten years ago."

If only we could have read one of those letters aloud, so passionate and convincing. But they had not survived.   Instead, we asked the preacher to read a poem Flo had written about her father after his death in 1938. She had been a prize-winning poet in her youth.

"Florence had a good mind. She was a quite a history buff," mused my father. "She worked with a group called Living Historians. They recorded oral interviews with senior citizens in the community. People who remembered how it was back when."

In her box of tapes, we had also found recordings of all of the Camp David Accords. Flo had been so excited by the prospect of peace between such old enemies. She loved history, I thought, but was irritated by our inability to learn from it. She would call me, hysterical about the state of the world, exhorting my generation to clean up the mess hers had made. At that moment I wasn't sure I could live without her ongoing critique.

The next day we all showed up at the funeral home in our most solemn black. My cousin Sandy strutted over, an adorable penguin in her three-piece suit and black bow tie. She was the only other dyke in the family, and ten years my senior.

"We'd like to see a menu, please," her sister, Sue Ellen, commanded. "Oh, pardon me. I thought you were the waiter."

My three cousins have always had to fight to be taken seriously. They're very short. Gail, the youngest at thirty-seven, was sometimes mistaken for a child and still endured periodic pats on the head. She resisted the impulse to pick fights with bigger people. Instead, she was obliged to draw on some defense mechanism other than intimidation. More often than not it was a rather off-beat sense of humor shared by all three cousins.

The six of us pallbearers — the cousins, my two sisters-in-law and I — were ushered into an anteroom. We only had a minute to start getting nervous before the preacher appeared, looking as if he'd gotten dressed in a hurry. An assistant, he said, would be in shortly to instruct us in proper pallbearer conduct.

"Is this the first time you've had all women?" I asked, hoping it was. "No, ma'am. We've had the women act as pallbearers with their husbands." He exited, without answering my question.

"Hello, girls," said the assistant brightly. I guessed his age at twenty-one. "First time we've had all girl pallbearers."

"We are all adult women here, and I think you can assume we would prefer to be addressed that way," said Gail, her jaw grinding.

"Yeah, okay." His smile showed a trace of sneer. "Now, when I give the cue, you will walk down the aisle arranged by height with the tallest first. The first pew to the left will be reserved for you."

"I don't think I like this," said Sandy, who is less than five feet tall. "Why should the tallest go first? This is institutionalized heightism." We nodded in agreement, straight-faced. The assistant was speechless.

"Why don't you just let us decide how to walk in," Sue Ellen suggested.

"Sure, okay," he shrugged, and left the room.

We laughed, partly at our little victory, and partly from nervousness. I'd been concerned about our collective ability to carry this coffin. Now, I could see in the faces of the other women a trace of doubt. I was a construction worker and weight lifter, confident of my physical strength, but I realized they probably had no idea of their ability. And none of us had ever lifted a coffin (how heavy were they?). My muscle-bound brother told me he had split his pants and thrown out his back lowering a friend's casket into the grave. Was it possible that we might fail at this task? I wanted bearing my mother's body to the grave to make me feel powerful and competent. But I couldn't do it myself. I needed the other women.

The service came off satisfactorily. None of us was terribly disappointed; U.S. Imperialism wasn't mentioned, but neither was God the Father, as I recall. My only surprise was the large number of people in attendance. I supposed there had been others in my mother's life besides me. Perhaps, if I hadn't been the exact center of her universe, I'd been a closely revolving planet.

As it turned out, we pallbearers only had to carry the casket a short distance, from the cart at the funeral parlor door to the hearse, then again from the hearse to the grave. The coffin, though cumbersome, was easily lifted. (Later I learned that Flo had weighed only sixty-eight pounds at her death.) Our main struggle was persuading the funeral parlor staff that we did not need help. They appeared, muscles flexed, each time we lifted or set down the casket. The men would then slide in silently and try to take the weight from us without our noticing. The constant effort to hold in my grief made it hard to fight this continuing battle, and my irritation grew with each encounter.

By the end of our sojourn they had gotten the point and we were allowed to set the casket on a platform on the grave. As we lowered the casket, the back end was a bit higher than the front. I felt the body shift, there was an unmistakable rap. Was that Flo's head hitting the end of the box? Suddenly it occurred to me that there might be a reason for the "tall in front, short in back" rule. I looked at my comrades and dismissed the idea. We'd been great.

Nine months later we returned to the same funeral home to bury Gerda. One of her last requests had been that the grand-daughters serve as her pallbearers. We were confident now, we'd had practice at this. And as we proudly grasped the casket's handles for the short walk down the church steps to the hearse, funeral attendants stepped in front and back of us. "Here, girls, we'll help," one said. "This is too heavy for you."

"Bug off," said Gail. We shook our heads in unison, elbowing them out of the way. At that moment I could feel Flo cheering us on and smiling.

ON PASSING

Laura Munter-Orabona

"*N*o lo creo, no lo creo!" . . . as they lowered the casket into the ground, her words came back to me in hot whispers, "*No lo creo!*" "Stay with me, Mami," I answered half aloud. My head jerked. I shifted in the chair, aware of others sitting quietly around me. I turned my gaze and let the grief slide from my face as I focused on the well-trimmed grass and the thin metal pole of the tent surrounding us.

Familia . . . my father, my brother, *titi* Chelin, *abuelito*, Lena, *la gente de mami*. Nearly strangers to me. *Tio* Luis had broken into tears when he entered the hospital and got a last look at my mother. I wasn't used to much emotion in men, in anyone. His sobs caught him in the middle. They took his breath and bent him in two next to her bed. Now at the funeral I felt their sideways glances. Their questioning looks. I could throw myself at the side of her grave like on TV. Would they understand then? How my tears lay deep beneath each layer of skin like buried cities . . . each with a woven tale . . . this was my grief when they took *mi* from you *mi tias* . . . snatched me from your arms . . . your music, the warmth *de mi tierra* . . . *la lengua de mi corazon* . . . and this is the grief as they took you Mami. How could they understand? I hadn't lived with them in so many years and in my new home I did not cry before strangers . . . especially family.

I did times tables in my head, like I did in Catholic school. Soon the familiar band of steel locked around my forehead like a tight hat. I had regained control.

"Thank you for the sparse gathering," I said to myself, relieved that my parents had quit their teaching jobs a year earlier and moved to this small Florida town. There were no neighbors, no teachers. At her gravesite, my anger would have sliced those people in two. Only the closest *familia* stood by. *Tio* Tonio . . . he looks just like my brother Kerry, I thought. Twenty years in small Michigan towns and I had never seen a person who looked like my family. We moved so often. We were always the new family in town. In those towns everyone was related to each other. Three last names would take up half of the population. Isolation is an odd thing. Seeing my mother's *familia*, seeing that I had once belonged in the midst of their laughter, their warmth, the music of their language, my language. Emotions collided within me like hands, gentle on my back, like a slap to my face. There was one sobbing woman whom I did not recognize. I welcomed her hysteria. The absurdity of a woman I had never seen before wailing at my mother's funeral tamed the hysteria within me.

"Gastritis," the doctor had said, and kept saying. Later he corrected his diagnosis, as though he'd merely forgotten a comma in the sentence, "Cancer of the lower intestines." It had spread: "Gastritis." It kept spreading: "Cancer." After the third surgery, I heard the doctor tell my father, "If it comes back, we'll just open her up and take it out again . . . all the lesions, looks like somebody took a bottle of glue and spread it all over her insides." The glasses sat straight on his angular nose, his hands were shoved deep in the pockets of a starched white coat. She was just another body to him, a woman and a Puerto Rican at that. Just another spic. "You don't know her," I wanted to scream. "She studied medicine just like you, at better schools than you, fluent in five languages, her father and the Governor called each other by nickname."

But here in the U.S., it didn't matter. It hadn't mattered. She'd tried to pack her lineage with the baggage and two small children as she left the island to rejoin her American husband, my father. But her aristocracy was of a crumbling class and did not survive the journey. It was lost in the translation and thrived only in the mind of my mother. The grandeur was recaptured in my daydreams, nurtured by her stories of fine houses with fountains in the middle, memories of the upper class in Old San Juan. Those stories were my weapons against the racism of small town people. "Hey half-nigger"—"In Puerto Rico, my people are rich;" "Hey little spic" — "They are doctors and lawyers, the whole town are their friends;" "Little slut" — "You are all dirt and too stupid to know it, my people matter." Her memories blossomed in my fantasies and held me together like the net of a fish trap.

As the illness chewed its way through Mami's body, my father prepared. The casket salesman sat in my father's living room. He spoke gently, efficiently, drew details of various boxes. He had placed catalogues and brochures neatly on the table. "Catafalque," he kept saying, not casket, not coffin, as though the unfamiliar term would ease the pain. With his head buried in his hands, my father began to cry. The tears slipped through openings between his fingers. I wanted to reach out and comfort him. But years of practice made me rise and drift into another room. Emotions were to be hidden. I heard the casket man comforting him, surprised at the tenderness and sincerity of the smooth salesman.

The last weeks with my mother filled me with emptiness. My emotions surrounded me like still air. I functioned as in a dream. I'd been flying back and forth from Michigan and hadn't seen her in a month. As I rounded the door to her hospital room, the sight of her ninety-pound body made me gasp. I tried to recover, but she'd seen. "Just a bag of bones," she said, shaking her head. For a moment the truth stood thick between us. As she sat up in bed, I noticed the deep red rinse gone from her hair. Soft braids hugged her head. The gray plaits gave an odd look of a little girl grown old too fast. Mami drew her head close to mine, focused through the sheath of drugs, "I'm going to lick this thing," she said in a feverish whisper, "I'm going to lick this thing."

My youngest brother visited the hospital rarely. Sitting silently, his anger and fear cast a sullen veil. He could barely speak to our mother. I was relieved when his visits stopped. "Don't be angry with the boys," Dad said, "It's hard for them." Kerry, her favorite son, came twice. On my last visit I glimpsed his inability to accept her dying. "She's just looking for sympathy," Kerry said. His high-pitched voice at thirty-two still held so much of his boyhood. "All we need to do is get her a ten-speed. She can get off her buns and ride." Later, after one of his visits, I'd seen him seated on a couch outside her room, clutching a Bible. He thumbed frantically through its thin frail pages and begged its testament to keep him strong.

She'd been a busy woman, giving us bits of time between preparing lesson plans, working on another degree, running a travel business.

In her heart she sought more than motherhood. *"Carumba, muchacha!"* she'd say, impatient with the child I was. Details of home finally gave way to other ambitions. I remember buttons popping off in school when the pins securing them on my dresses would no longer hold. But I wore her achievements like shiny medals, my chest puffed out. "My mother is working on her doctorate," I'd say to my friend's mother as she mended my clothes when I'd spend the night. I knew most of their parents had only finished high school, if that.

I savored the times she spent with me. Once, she showed me the first crocus in her garden, deep violet pushed through soil to meet the new warmth of Michigan spring. I'd wanted to bury myself deep in the black earth, have her hands knead me around the roots of the brilliant spring flower. Deep in the soil, deep in my mother's touch.

In the family album, I remember her pictured tiny against the sea, but not diminished, standing high and glamorous on the cliff nearby, wearing white slacks and tailored blouse. She was so fashionable then, living in D.C. That pride and arrogance burst from the black and white edges of the photo. Her eyes stared straight out of that flat picture past me. My mother's life had always been as vast with promise as the ocean calling to her back.

The end was difficult. I planned on staying only two weeks. My bags filled the trunk of my father's car. He had taken me to the hospital to say goodbye. I was relieved to be leaving. The well-honed racism of this Florida town scared me. "They only let black people move here two years ago," my father said. Their outright bigotry dwarfed a northern brand of his own.

We left the hospital, headed toward the airport. I was so eager to leave, I felt the heaviness starting to lift with each mile. "Can't he drive faster?" I thought. I wanted to outrun the truth, which was pulling at the edge of my senses. I wanted the comfort of my friends, my home. I looked over, my father seemed tight and nervous, maybe scared. I knew I was safe. I knew he wouldn't ask me to stay. I wanted to run from this hellish ending. The neck of my shirt was wet. I moved in the seat and felt my shirt and legs clinging to the plastic. I remember her... so thin, frail, only a matter of time. I knew I could not leave, but

I didn't want to speak. "Take me back, Dad," I finally said. I felt grief. I felt relief. I saw the tension leave his forehead, felt him breathe a sigh. We both knew that if I left that day, I would not see my mother again. But we could not speak the words.

The next day I moved through the house, cooking, doing laundry. I noticed the plants were dying. I was stunned I had not noticed before. They seemed to scream out to me. The lonely remains, the dry soil, the crunchy leaves echoed a low moan that was building in me. That morning before going back to the hospital, I emptied all the pots in a shed out back. It was as though each plant was seeding the loss deeper within me. I felt my heart open to the sadness. "I'm going to lick this thing," I heard her whisper. She'd always won, wielding her self-assured brilliance, her arrogance and privilege like a shield against the mentality of those small Michigan towns. But the dying plants brought the truth gently home. The next day while my father was away, I packed some of my mother's things. I moved slowly, carefully folding all the brilliant-colored clothes that were hardly popular at the time. Oranges, purples, I packed methodically, mechanically. The stack of boxes grew taller, the closets emptier. I could not touch the rows and rows of knick-knacks. At moments, my hands would stop on a familiar piece of clothing, draw it close to me. Unable to say goodbye, I caressed the smooth material with my hands, imprinting her memory on my fingertips.

The last week at the hospital, my father and I were unable to speak comfort. We moved through anger, despair and disbelief as though passing each other on an open stairway, each locked in our own grief, set in our own direction. My grandfather would quietly bring *arroz con pollo* and *platanos* stuffed with *queso blanco* to the house. Each day Mami would crave an old familiar food. Days later a crate from Puerto Rico might arrive packed with smells that stirred a deep memory in me. I was five years old at the market place in Santurce, nose-high to the warm food wrapped in banana leaves. I watched my mother's hand reach for the *tamal,* the *pasteles.* But here in the hospital, three years of chemotherapy and heavy sedatives robbing her of taste and other senses, she would try the *tamarindo,* shake her head, ask for the *leche de avena,* shake her head again.

She floated in and out of consciousness. *"No lo creo,* I don't believe it," she said over and over again. "I don't believe it. They're chasing me, stop them."

I wanted to comfort her, to reach her, to be the one to ease the pain. To comfort her as she passed. Finally, the tubes were gone from her arms, from her nose, no more Demerol, no more Talwin, no more liquid food. "Take them out," she said. And slowly starving, she drifted home, returned to her motherland, spoke only the language of her heart. *"No lo creo. No lo creo."* She spoke many things I can't remember, words I didn't remember, words I didn't understand. The familiar forgotten words filled me with a mourning song as they lifted her from me. And my anger rose.

I don't know at what point I had turned from my native language. "Talk English or don't talk at all," my father had said as my brother and I passed from the warmth of *mi familia's* arms, from the island of my birth, to my father's snow-covered home. My mother left my father years earlier, me in her belly, my brother on her arm. "Talk English or don't talk at all." I stopped speaking for two years they said. "We thought you were damaged ... we were going to see doctors, then one day you said, 'bubba gum.'"

Maybe Dad thought he was helping. Maybe he felt threatened that we could leave him with conversation. Years later they both wanted us to learn to undo the error. Then they decided we would speak only Spanish at dinner. *"Mantequilla, por favor."* My father had studied Spanish that summer in Kalamazoo. "Your accent is horrible," my mother would snap. I would think of the dopey man on TV, *"Si, Senor."* Oh we knew Spanish, my brother and I. We knew *zapato,* we knew *carajo,* we knew *mierda.* Then one day at school, in my third grade class, my father showed up to teach us Spanish. He was a music teacher, but they didn't know. "Isabel, *te gustas albondigas?"* and together, thirty seven-year-olds would answer, *"No, no me gusto albondigas."* But now standing mute at my mother's passing, Mami calling out to me in terror, calling out to me in our native tongue, I felt awakened in the middle of a rape. Each foreign word another thrust. Awakening me to the long-buried loss of *cultura, mi corazon. "No lo creo. No lo creo,"* she said. *"Mami, no entiendo,"* I answered. My rage rising, I understood the lunatic gunning wildly through a crowd.

The end came quickly. I sent my father home early that night. He sat solemnly in the chair across from her hospital bed, staring at the thin frame of the woman he'd shared a bed with for thirty-two years. His eyes were bloodshot and glassy and though mother had asked him not to come drunk, it hardly mattered now. Her eyes were glassed-over, sight gone, her body shrunk a little each day. I abandoned the anger at my mother's lost request. I walked across the room. "Dad?" I placed my hand gently on his knee, not wanting to startle him. "Why don't you go home. There is no need for both of us to stay." He resisted at first. I don't recall what made him agree. "I'll call," I said. He needed some sleep, needed a break from this bleak white room and I was relieved he was gone.

It was nine o'clock at night. Alone in her room, I felt peaceful at first. But the unrest grew quickly. I switched channels on the TV, tried to read, walked to the window, listened to the cicadas night chatter, buzzing like bad neon. Soon the walls began to argue for space, closing in on me, opening too wide. I paced, looked at the clock . . . 9:30 . . . listened closely for my mother's breathing. Earlier that evening the nurse had come by. "Why don't you pack some of her things," she said. A bit surprised I accepted the brown bag she handed me. I packed some things, her toothbrush, her Bible, some earrings. When I was through, a dozen roses my grandmother had sent adorned the top of the brown sack. I remembered my mother's story of Abuelita's death in Puerto Rico. It had been a long painful illness and toward the end the nuns would sit in constant vigil. They prayed through the morning, *"Prego por nosotros ahora, y en la hora de nuestra muerte, Amen."* They prayed through the long still night. I imagined their heavy habits of devotion, their soft fingers caressing the beads, with the rhythm of their steady chant, *"Dios de salve Maria,"* filling the room. And I longed for them as I longed for my homeland, for its way of life, for its way of death . . . .

The minutes passed so slowly and here in this foreign place, I knew no thought to ease the terror, no inner voice to quiet the restless. I could not sit with the slow hand of time, my only companion. My mother had taught me to pray in Spanish. *"En el nombre del padre, del hijo, del santos cristos . . ."* showed me how to make the tiny cross with thumb and forefinger. But my thoughts rested on the Valium on her dresser. I had given up drugs since I'd seen her pain. Measuring it against mine, drugs seemed cowardly and frail. Living daily with my father's alcoholism had reseeded a bitter belief. "I will never be like him. My life is too precious and I have more pride."

The small hospital cot they'd brought for me was next to the wall. I looked again at the clock. Habit stronger than pride I slipped the pills into my mouth. I crawled into the stiff white sheets of the cot, letting the pills cradle me.

I heard her cough in the night, gasp for air. I wanted to sit up, to go to her. But the pull of the drug held me to the soft bed like an old lover. I rolled back to the comfort. "Get up, go to her, you should help," I heard the voice softly as I heard her cough again; but, guilt and compassion nudged only softly. I did not move.

The nurse shook me gently at first, then a little more firmly. She was so far away. Let me sleep. Was it morning? I searched through the darkness. "Your . . . mother . . . has . . . passed." The words stung even through the thick wrap of the drug. When had she left? I had been laying next to her, just Mami and me, our bodies rising and falling like the calm roll of the sea. When had she grown still? When had her breath stopped answering mine?

I arose, walked slowly to where she lay. I touched my mother's cheek, caressing the still warm peaceful skin. I had wanted to hold her hand as she died. But she was gone. Death cradled her in its arms, quieted the voices, rested the visions.

It was 5:20 in the morning, 1951, Santurce, Puerto Rico. Mami, you brought me in and the sea surrounded me like the waters of your womb. It was 5:15 A.M., a Florida town, Seventh-day Adventist hospital. I caressed your cheek. You had passed from me.

Mother, he buried you in a thin brown nightie, *Amour* stitched in thick white letters across the bosom. The birthstones of your children hung around your neck. "I thought this would be all right," he'd said, shy at the intimacy, as he showed me the neatly laid out gown and carefully placed jewelry. I could not tell him I wanted to fold you soft in blankets beneath a blooming magnolia. I wanted to bury you at its base, let its roots cradle you safe, cradle you warm.

Mami, you were the thread reaching through me to the island, my voice on every visit, my memory, my reminder. I thought I could not return without you. But I am just now finding my own way home.

ALONE

Christine Moriarty

I played pool the night my mother died. I was eighteen and had left the forty-three year old man with whom I lived, and began living with the man I eventually married. But we were fighting a lot and I felt enormously guilty about leaving my mother alone, so I told her I would move back home.

I was staying the night at Mother's and we were watching television. Maurice, the forty-three year old Ph.D. anthropologist from Alabama called. I don't know how he knew I was at my mother's. He had a way of ferreting out my weaknesses and taking advantage of them.

"I want to see you," he said. "Let's go play pool."

"I can't leave my mother alone," I said with my hand cupped over the phone. "She's sick."

"You've left her alone for the last year," Maurice said."What difference does a couple of hours make? We'll go to the bar right down the street."

True, true. I had left her alone for the last year since the death of my father. True, true. I was bored spending a full evening with her. She didn't talk much. She just sat there looking sad. True, true. The bar was only a block away.

"Okay," I said, with only a few seconds hesitation. "But I don't want any pressure from you."

"No pressure, no hype," he promised, and we hung up.

Maurice met my father before he died and he knew my mother quite well. They didn't know we had lived together. Since I had finished high school at sixteen, my parents figured they didn't have to worry about anything I did. They were too old and too tired to fight with me.

Maurice drove up in his convertible MG. He had that stupid black beret on his head when he came to the door. We sat and talked with my mother for a while. "I don't want you to walk upstairs until we get back," I told her, like a mother to a child. "We'll be back in an hour, so promise me you won't try to go upstairs."

She agreed meekly.

Maurice left the MG parked in front of the house and we walked to the bar.

Pool was one of my passions then. We rapidly drank several beers, ate the free popcorn and played a game of pool. The grease and salt from the popcorn, the blue chalk and the baby powder from the pool cue were wiped on my faded jeans. The salt taste stayed in my mouth.

On the way home. Maurice tried to hold my hand and tell me how much he still loved me. I told him I couldn't handle the responsibility right then.

I turned the key in the door and knew immediately that something was wrong. Mother was gone from the green chair. I could hear moaning from upstairs. She was in the throes of a fatal heart attack and there was nothing I could do.

Her heart had broken when my father died. She shifted around alone in the old house. She never asked me to move back in to take care of her, but her pleading eyes haunted me whenever I left her alone. She had given me a false alarm a few months earlier. She phoned complaining of chest pains. Maurice and I drove like madmen from our northside apartment to her southside house, even though I had several brothers and sisters living within a few miles of her house.

We rushed in the door to find her sitting at the table reading the paper.

"Would you like some tea?" she said calmly. We had tea and cookies and kept her company for a few hours, which was all she really needed.

No false alarm this time. Shortly before the end, lying in my arms, she gave her deathbed confession.

"I can't live," she said simply. Her life sentence of sadness and despair was ending. Mine was only beginning.

PRIVATE RITUALS
A Prose Meditation In Five Stories

Jyl Lynn Felman

I. Milk

My family adjusts in silence as we let in the irrevocable knowledge of my mother's Parkinson's. It is a neurological disorder, a chemical deficiency in the brain that tightens the nerves, causing rigidity in the body. It is not hereditary, not environmental. No one knows the origin. The body slowly deteriorates into total dependency; it cannot support itself. There is eventually no life to give life.

The last time I saw my mother was in Boston, in the morning, a Thursday morning around 9:15 in her hotel room. I am dressed, full of health, and look forward to our time alone, without my father. As I brush my hair one more hundredth time, pulling it longer because she has never liked my hair short — she sees it as a reaction to my gender, and a rejection of her womanhood— the phone in my room rings.

My father calls, wanting to make sure I order decaffeinated coffee for her since she cannot drink coffee in the morning or the L-dopa will not take. I have only ordered coffee for both of us. I immediately I feel bad, how could I be so insensitive, not to know intuitively that coffee for her in the morning is out. I must have known. When I call in our breakfast order, I stutter ordering the coffee. Ignoring my own message to myself, I say, "Two, enough coffee for two."

I overhear my father trying to find out if she wants skim milk.

"Edith, do you want skim milk?"

"Milk, yes, I have to have milk in the morning."

"I know you have to have milk in the morning, but do you want skim milk?"

"Yes, get me enough milk for the cereal and the pills."

"Edith, you're not listening, does the milk have to be

skim?"

"I want a glass and a half, enough also for the cereal."

I listen to this through the phone, embarrassed for him, hurting for her, humiliated for me. I should not be hearing what is between them, husband and wife, no room for a daughter here. Then I realize they have no idea that I am a partner in their conversations while they work out the milk, they forget I am present at the other end hearing everything.

"Dad, I ordered cream, half and half, extra."

"She ordered half and half; is that okay?"

"I need enough milk for the pills and the cereal."

I hang up the phone shaking: no one said the Parkinson's makes talking on the phone to healthy people difficult, no one said Parkinson's makes a giant hole inside the whole family. I have no idea what I ordered, whether or not there will be enough milk — cream, for the cereal, the pills, and for my own coffee.

I will drink my coffee black this morning, and from now on; so that there will always be enough milk for my mother. I leave my room for an intimate morning alone with her. I crave to be the daughter.

II. Waiting

As I knock on their door, I know with sudden clarity that I am not prepared for what is on the other side. I want to run back to the elevator, have breakfast alone with myself. My own good health, my abundant relationship with the world terrifies me as I hear my father walk towards the door.

She is lying down, propped up on three pillows with the blankets pulled all the way to her chin. She has no neck. My mother's eyes are closed; her face is tight with the Parkinson's mask, and her arms — without motion — are buried somewhere inside the covers. "I am so cold," she says, in a voice that is not hers, and that I barely hear above the news.

This morning my father is handsome; dressed in a suit, clean, fresh shaven, rugged, full of color, the red of life. He stands in front of the TV, listening to the morning news.

"Here's something for you." He hands me the paper.

I sit down to read the headlines, open the paper then realize what I have just done. Closed them both out.

[53]

"I am so cold, can you get me another blanket?" I think she is dying. I put the paper down, fold it back as though it was never opened and wait. Then I remember — the medicine has not yet begun to take. It is only 9:10, and it takes at least twenty minutes to work.

"When did you take the pill?"

"9:00."

I stand up to turn the volume down. I can't stand the noise and feel sure it is blocking the medication from taking. I am enraged that he has the TV on. Why can't he sit with her, hold her in his arms until the pill takes? But he can't, not this morning. I remind myself that I started to read the paper. It's almost twenty past. Soon, she'll sit up; we'll be alone; she will be the mother and I, the daughter.

"Yesterday I had to send the food back, the medicine didn't take, and I couldn't even answer the door," she whispers.

We don't answer her. We don't even look at each other. We act like she is not talking to us: who is she talking to? He's ready to leave for his meeting. I hug him.

Does he kiss her goodbye? I feel sure I would remember, if he bent his head to her face on top of three pillows, kissing her while she waits for the medicine to work. As though his single kiss to her heart could start the medicine running life through her blood. Today he does not kiss her goodbye.

I wait.

It is 9:30, the food arrives, she begins to sit up. How will she get to the table that has just been rolled into the room. How will she eat. What she will drink? There are two pots on the table. One of them has a red ribbon on the handle. "The ribbon is the decaf," the waiter says, closing the door. I look for the milk.

Then she starts to move for the first time since I knocked on the door thirty minutes ago. In her movement, I am exhausted. There is no room for illness and health to coexist: there is only illness.

III. Praying

She sits up slowly. I cannot believe how little, doll-like, she has become. I look for the woman in my mother. She has clothed herself in a pale yellow nightie that ties in a bow at the neck. She always wears night clothes that hide her womanhood and her strength.

A collar of white lace circles her neck; short, puffy sleeves trimmed to match the white lace protect her shoulders, the tops of her arms. She has a hundred of these gowns, in every color they look the same: light blue, sea green, salmon pink. I never like them, only that they feel soft to the touch assuages me. Now in illness, the pale yellow gown makes my mother a child. We haven't yet sat down for breakfast.

My mother is cold; the cold she feels is not the temperature of her body, but of her soul. I look for another blanket. I want to open a window, turn the air conditioner on, go outside. Breathe. At the table near the bed I sit down and remove the metal cover from my eggs. On the plate, beads of water surround my food; the eggs are wet from the heat.

For the first time this morning I look at her face; her eyes are closed. I think she is praying; she is only trying to swallow. And then her head starts to shake. That is the Parkinson's tremors, small, fast hyperkinetic movements of the head, the hands, the wrist; movements that look elegant, articulate and planned on Katharine Hepburn, make my mother look as if she is forever saying no.

"Do you want juice, fresh squeezed? It's good for you. I drink juice, orange juice every day." I despise my benevolent voice. She shakes her head. Is it a yes-shake or a no-shake? I pour both of us juice, hoping she doesn't want hers so I can have more. The illness makes me selfish, wanting more, extra, all the time.

My father, how does he do it: how does he stay with her? He never says anything: about her, about him, about the two of them together. I have got to find out how they are doing. If they are not doing well, she will never make it. My rage is back; his silence infuriates me. We are all ill with the Parkinson's and we know it. She has the tremors; we feel them, like the earth, quaking.

Still we have not eaten, either of us, anything. I have got to eat or I will lose my composure completely. She is totally consumed with the act of making herself comfortable. "What do you do when no one is around? How do you get up in the morning?"

"Slowly, very slowly." Her eyes are open: she looks straight ahead as though she is actually looking at something. I look straight ahead, too. I see nothing. Nothing is there. It is the mask: the Parkinson's mask that keeps the feelings inside, the face empty.

I tell myself to ignore it, pretend we are looking at each other and talk. Talk to her. Find some words. Then eat. Both of us must eat. I pick my arm up from my lap and reach for the orange juice: each movement an effort, I imitate her without knowing it.

IV. Strawberries

Her body slides into the chair towards the floor. I do not know what to do. "Do you want to eat in bed? I can roll the table over to the bed?" She shakes her head no; she is only half in the chair. I taste the warm, fresh-squeezed orange juice on my lips; my mouth is completely dry. I divide my eggs, put half on her plate. She is deformed; her entire body contorts.

I look. I cannot be afraid to look, but I must not stare. She is trying to open a plastic container that is taped shut. I am going to be sick; her fingers will not bend around the container. I freeze. What does my father do? No one has told me what to do.

I smile, talk loud, and do not stare. Only my mother is not deaf; she just can not hold the plastic, taped-shut container long enough to open it. I am angry that she taped it shut. I force myself not to ask her why she taped the top shut. Then I know, without having to ask. She tapes the container closed so that she does not spill the contents over everything. If she drops the container she cannot clean up the mess by herself. We have no way out of this maze.

"What is in there that you want?" I stall for time, hoping she will be able to open the lid by herself.

"Bran."

"Bran?" I have never known my mother to eat natural foods, fibers or fresh herbs.

"I am totally constipated." She is crying. "All the time. The medicine blocks my bowels."

Silently I take the container from her rigid hands, open it, pour the bran into a bowl and swallow slowly, reminding myself to breathe. I wish someone else could be here with me, to see. I cannot see all of this alone. I do not want to know that my mother, at fifty-eight, has not had a bowel movement for days.

She pours the cream into the bowl. Nothing spills. Certain movements come with ease; there is no explanation. She holds the spoon with a fist, like a child learning to eat by herself for the first time. We were never allowed to hold our silverware in fists. We were taught perfectly, flawless manners. My mother — her hand in a fist — brings a spoonful of plain, brown bran up to her mouth.

"How can you eat that plain?" I know from my friends to sprinkle bran on fruit, in a salad, or add it to orange juice and stir. But not to eat it plain. It makes you choke. For decoration, I cut the strawberries on my plate into small, bite-size pieces. She is crying.

I put the strawberries into her bowl. Then I cut a half moon piece of lime melon into the strawberries. Finally, gently, I take the spoon out of her fist, stir the fruit into the bran, and put the spoon back into her fist. Then I eat my eggs. She has not stopped crying. I put my fork down. I wait. It is impossible to eat while she cries.

"Try the bran now, you'll be surprised at the taste."

She is eating. I eat. I watch her eat. I want to know if she can taste the food, if she gets any pleasure from the sensuousness of eating or if the enormous energy it takes to eat, takes away the pleasure of tasting, chewing, being alive. How long can she live with the Parkinson's?

V. Rigidity

I must find out, learn the details, know the life of the illness consuming my mother. Today I will ask questions. I will start to find out what it is like to be her and then will decide what it is I am going to say to her in the end, about her, about me, about us.

Her head falls to the right. I think she is sleeping, exhausted from the effort it takes to eat. "The m-e-d-i-c-i-n-e is wearing o-o-f-f-f." Her body is still. She points with her eyes to her pills. Each pill should last for two hours. We have only been sitting for an hour. It is too soon for the medication to slow down.

I hand her the pills, not knowing if she can take them herself, or if I need to open her mouth, and lay the pills on her tongue with a little water. This question I do not have the courage to ask because I am not ready for the answer. Instead I wait.

Her entire face wrinkles in pain. She cannot swallow. I want to take the pills for her. At the same time, I cannot absolutely believe that she is trying hard enough. How could it be that she cannot swallow? I do not say anything. This is uniquely hers, a private ritual; the healthy do not understand the rituals of the sick.

She knows what to do next. Somehow, within the ritual her muscles will relax, release their choking grip and the pills will slide down her throat into her stomach. In twenty minutes — thirty at most — she will sit again upright and we will talk. It will be as though the rigidity never happened, that I imagined my mother could not swallow her medication.

Why is it so hard for me to believe her when she tells me she cannot swallow, cannot even move? Have I always not believed her? Or is it now, only because I see her alive in front of me, going through the motions of the living, acting like I act, doing what I do, that I stop believing her? The fight between the healthy and the sick is a fight for credibility.

The illness takes from my mother her credibility. She ceases to be a believable person to me, someone with whom I trust my vision of the world. I have no right as a healthy person to take away her integrity. This is true. And yet I am reluctant to treat her as her own witness.

My mother is the bearer of her own reality, bearing into the world of the living the painful, unmitigated truth about the Parkinson's. The struggle for credibility between the healthy and the sick is the struggle for a common language. We have no common languages, we have no language. We have no words.

THE PACT

Rose Mary Fandel

It was when they told my mother she was dying of liver cancer that we made our pact. A pact to guarantee her respectful passing. My mother had carried out such a pact with her father who died of cancer in 1948. I was aware of such agreements all my life. The promises are as intricate as the individuals involved.

My parents called me to come get them at the hospital, and my mother signed herself out. For the hospital staff this was an act of insanity. A grieving family's unacceptance of death. For us it was the only decision to make. She belonged home, her incision would heal faster there, it was normal for her to be home.

The elderly often lose control over their lives at crucial moments. My mother didn't wish this to happen with her death. She swore my father to noninterference and asked me to share her death and to be partners with her again in birth. I believe the pact is one made between loved ones since the beginning of time. My mother's request was simple. The first part was for me to care for her at home until she died. The second part came because both of us wanted nothing to do with the hospital's prolonging of life beyond the wishes of an individual. So when the pain became so great she couldn't bear it, and it diminished the quality of her life, she would tell me and then I would medicate her deeply so that she'd slip easily into her next life. The rest of her request concerned the washing and oiling of her body after death and her wish to be buried in pants.

Four years later, Mom began to lose ground. I moved in on a Wednesday as she began this life's release. I was so sure I could honor our pact, and I felt so brave. Mom and I talked in the wispy words that were all she could manage, and I matched them as her partner in this last dance. She was not understood any longer by others. The hospital bed was in the living room only a chair's width from the couch where I slept. This space became our last world together. I sat and held her hand the way she held my hand when I was a little girl.

Thursday night at 11 P.M. she asked for the medicine. It took me by surprise. I knew what we were doing, but with her presence during all the planning I had slid into this with such comfort that I forgot that our goal was to facilitate her leaving.

The fear hit me with such force. I denied her request. For seconds that might have been minutes my mind reeled in a world devoid of past or present, solely filled with the feeling of loss and being lost forever. My mother's voice yelled my name like I was a three-year-old being held within the confines of the yard by her tone alone — and I turned to the task.

Arrangements for the drug laudanum had been made to kill the pain. I placed the call to our hospice nurse who then got the drug ordered and delivered within the hour. I began by giving Mom four times the regular dose and continued the doses every hour. Mom dreamed time away, waking only once in the morning to pray. She wasn't really present when I did her morning care. Her body's internal noises had stopped at 4 A.M., a sign of imminent death.

Just before her death, Mom was fully conscious for many minutes. There were lots of goodbyes because the house was full of friends and family. Mom's god-niece and a friend came to the house at the last moment. Mom had stopped breathing and with their entrance had started up again. I felt that the commotion in the room had called her back from her journey toward death and new life. I leaned over her, saying I loved her and we all would be fine and she should go on. She stopped breathing. At noon on Friday, June 15, she began her new life, in her living room surrounded by friends and family at her chosen time.

This is a never-ending story. I found out that Mom is still present. I didn't have to be afraid of never having contact again. Though I must admit she doesn't respond to trivial matters anymore, and it was easier to capture her time when I could just ring her up on the phone. Yet during a tornado soon after her death, I was sitting in my car, chanting, and I felt my mother's hand on my shoulder and heard her voice say, "It'll be okay." Not all our exchanges are at such critical times. I get a slice of her every once in awhile and hear her comments now and again, mostly at happy times when I'm doing something she liked.

I still grieve and miss her kisses and hugs. But anguish and fear of death are no longer the fearful mystery in my life or future. That is the gift Mom gave me through our pact's completion. HAPPY BIRTHDAY MOM.

WHEN MOUNTAINS MOVE

Joan Connor

When my father enters the kitchen, my mother smoothly shifts to another topic. I have just finished asking her if her scalp itches. Her hair is growing back — a gray as soft as mown hay left weathering in an October field. Silver thatch.

"Oh no," she says. "Never let a dog bully you. They sniff fear. If Toby acts afraid, just tell him to keep walking right on by." Only her finger twisting a shock of her short hair betrays her insincerity. "That's the only way Toby will overcome his fear of that dog."

Toby is my two year old son. The dog is imaginary. My mother's elbows press against the nicked surface of the kitchen table. She rests her chin on her hands, affecting casualness. Her head sways slightly in the hammock of her interlaced fingers. "Hi, dear," she greets my father breezily and smiles. But he stares at her, suspicious and baffled. He stands in the door-frame, his hair uncombed, his shirttail untucked, his elbows cocked — sharp as accusations. "What are you two talking about?" he asks abruptly.

"Conquering the fear of dogs," my mother says. She sips at her now cold cup of coffee. Its surface shimmers with an iridescent skim, floating like a gas stain on a rain-slicked parking lot. She swallows.

"The hell you were," my father snaps. The tail of his shirt flutters as he pivots and bolts from the room.

My mother sighs. I smile in sympathy. It is all I find to offer her now. When Mom called to share her latest doctor's report with me, I packed up my sympathy, my bags, Toby. "I'm going to stay with my mother." I told Curt. "Perhaps your parents would rather be alone right now," he said. But I knew my father. My mother would need me. Three weeks ago, my mother decided, "No more chemo."

My father raged for a week. "Suicide," he said. "It's

suicide plain and simple. How can you do this to me? To you?"

"Do what?" my mother answered. "I'm not doing anything. I've just decided not to take action. No more chemo."

Her resolve confounds him. My father flaps around the house, bewildered by her courage or cowardice; he is not certain which. I want to extend sympathy. But when he brushes back his bafflement like the gray hair from his eyes, he stares at my mother and me, his eyes scouting the trail of our conversation for the unmistakable sign of our conspiratorial morbidity — the bent twig, the clear print that will lead him to us in our guilt — treed.

My mother pushes herself up from the table and pours her coffee down the sink drain. She reaches for a dishcloth and dabs at a spill on the white porcelain. She keeps rubbing the spot long after it is dry while she stares out the window at the jagged ring of perse mountains.

Her voice startles me. "You know, your father's acting as if I'm leaving him for another man," she says, then laughs a short, embarrassed laugh. "I think he's jealous."

"He feels excluded," I say.

My mother stands very still. "It's good practice," she says. "Death is exclusive." In the tangy, autumn air, the words sting. I try to warm my hands on the porcelain mug, now cold. My mother continues, "He thinks it's all you and I ever talk about, death and dying. He thinks it's all I think about."

Actually my father would be surprised. We talk mainly about life, about Toby, or some memory that we've refined over the years into a one-liner sure to provoke an easy laugh. Remember that time when we lived in that tract development and Dad entered the wrong house, yelled, "Honey, Sugar Bear's home." Remember the time we took the train all the way to New York to pick up the car and you forgot the keys . . . remember. But these memories have an urgency now that belies the easy laugh.

My mother interrupts my memories with a sentence almost clairvoyant. "Of course," she says, still staring out the window, "your father isn't all wrong. My life is about death now." And then she snaps the dish rag briskly as if irritated by her own melodrama. "Let's sit outside. It's warmer outside this time of year, and there's precious little sun in the mountains anyway."

Toby is up from his nap. My mother and I sit in recliners on the front lawn chair watching him scuffle through the leaves tangled in the high grass. Dad's let the lawn go. No point mowing this time of year, he says, first frost will be any night now. He's right; its nearness tingles in the air with the irrepressible edginess of intuition. The trees sense it. Squirrels bury acorns in the meadow. But the mountains shunt the omens aside, shoulder up, purple, against the sky. They can bear what winter hurls at them. Permanent, proud, powerful, they shun time. Green, purple, white, they bear up.

I glance at my mother. Her eyes, clear and dark, reflect the sky. Clouds scud across them. I feel the cold of the ground hunkering below the web of the recliner. But the late afternoon sun warms my chest, my arms. For a second, I am almost glad to be here in the only place that has ever signified home; then I remember why I am here.

"I love it here this time of year," I say aside to my mother. "It's so beautiful . . . something to do with the slant of light."

My mother flashes me a look of impatience. I wonder if I should change the subject, but I press on. "The way the light falls, so purple. Light, air and color seem all one element."

My mother closes her eyes tight and puckers her mouth with irritation. But I can't stop talking; survival suddenly depends on talking. "I wish Toby could grow up here," I say. "It's such a great place to raise kids. Outdoors where they can run. No one they can bother."

My mother jerks up, snaps the back of her recliner straight. "Stop talking nonsense," she says. "We all wish. Wish. Wish. Wish. Wishes," she nearly sneers. "Why is everyone so wishy?"

I shade my eyes, hiding them from her. I don't know the answer.

"Wishy," she repeats. "Wishy, wishy, wishy-washy."

I pause, then free-associate, "If wishes were horses, beggars could ride." Nonsense language. She speaks it.

She laughs, a long natural laugh, and I join her. Toby looks up and laughs, too. He toddles toward us, his hands full of plucked grass, and throws the grass at my mother's legs. She flicks the blades aside with a cursory brush of her fingertips and asks, "Why doesn't anyone know how to talk to me anymore? Why especially now?"

My eyes sting. "No one knows what to say, Mom. No one knows the right response."

"Right response," she parrots. "There is no right response to death. You make it up as you go along."

Again I have no answer for her. I huddle, uneasily silent, back in my chair. Her eyes darken so blue, so purple that she could hide in their shade. They shine with privacy, a turning inward like that which glints in pregnant women's eyes — as if all meaning were interior.

"At least your father gets angry," my mother complains, but her voice is mild. "At least your father reacts, confronts the hard truth of all this." She picks a blade of grass from her pant leg, begins chewing it. "You always were evasive, even as a child."

I want to shout at her. "This isn't evasion. This is empathy. Talk my ear off. Cut me with resentments hidden and honed for thirty or forty years. But just tell me everything and let me feel it too." But I do not. She's got enough on her mind. I merely watch Toby trundle into a pile of leaves banked against the snow fence. Dad didn't bother to roll the fence up this spring.

My mother's right hand curves like a visor over her eyes as she watches Toby. "He doesn't remind me much of you," she says.

I nod. "Still, it's odd," I say, my tone self-consciously neutral, conversational. "When Toby was born, the instant I saw his face, I recognized him. I knew his face instantly as I know my own. It sounds impossible, but I knew him like someone I'd grown up with all my life."

My mother's hand drops from her eyes. The cords in her neck tense. Her eyes fix on me, alert. "What?" she asks. "What did you say?" Her eyes so bright they scorch me. "I only said that when Toby was born I felt as if . . . . "

She nods her head vigorously, cutting me off. "Yes," she says, "that is what it's like since I decided to stop the chemo, every instant feels like that, prescient somehow, already known. Dying feels like that, the unknown known." As she says this, she folds her hands in her lap, a gesture of satisfaction, completeness.

I close my eyes in relief and panic — relief that, at last, I know we can talk about IT directly, and panic that I will not find the courage, that our time, what may be our last time together, will roll away from me.

"I feel," my mother's voice slices through my panic, "I feel like an embarrassment."

My back stiffens. I listen to my mother's voice as I open my eyes. Toby tosses about in the leaves. His small sky rains yellow maple leaves. Then they land, he scoops them up and tosses them over and over again.

"I feel like I've done something dreadfully embarrassing, indelicate, in choosing not to have any more chemo." My mother's voice rises and falls, rhythmically, like a voice at prayer. "Your father thinks I have chosen to die, but I have not. I have only chosen no more chemo. It makes me so tired, unnaturally tired, not like illness or fatigue." She continues, "I cannot choose, none of us can choose, not to die. We die. But I can choose not to drag myself around, bone-tired and too spent to care. I can choose to remember my last days . . . not that I'll be able to remember . . . I mean; I don't know. " She falters in momentary confusion, then continues. "It's my decision. And I think that decision embarrasses your father and you."

"No, Mom," I start to protest. But she hushes me with a raised palm.

"But that isn't what matters. What matters is that I embarrass myself, like I've let myself down, lugging this old body around, this body that has failed me. My mind. My will. This split in me . . . I just . . . deep embarrassment, not fear. That's all. I just wanted you to know that. I really can't explain. It's just embarrassment of body."

I cannot look at my mother. I do not think I can say anything to her. But I hear my voice, a little choked and strangled, but still my voice, telling her, "Mom, Christmas Eve, last Christmas Eve, Curtis left the gate unlatched. I didn't know it was unlatched. I was carrying boxes out to the van. I thought Toby was inside playing with some measuring cups in the kitchen. Then I saw his back, just a glimpse disappear, disappear through the gate. Time shriveled up. I dropped the packages and screamed. Then my legs found themselves running, stretching out. I reached the sidewalk. All this happening in a heart beat. No time to think, only to watch Toby's legs fly off the curb into the cars. Hundreds of cars. I looked, saw the cars bearing down on Toby. And I screamed and waved my arms. A yellow Checker cab, a bus, a red Mustang, I remember the red Mustang, a motorcycle . . . . I could have rushed in. I could have dodged into the traffic after Toby. But I did not. I could not. Something prevented me. I ran back and forth along the sidewalk, my arms flapping, my voice clucking, 'Oh, my God. Oh, my God.' But I did not try to cross the lanes of traffic. I heard horns, the screech of brakes. My thighs bumped against the fenders. My arms wrapped around Toby. I cried and would never look in the mirror again without knowing that I wasn't who I'd thought I was. I can pretend I was paralyzed by fear, but I distinctly remember pacing back and forth along the road. I made a choice of myself over my son." My voice winds down. My hands wipe at my wet, salty face. Then I raise my head, my mother's eyes attack mine with a clear ferocity.

"'Then you know it all," she says. Her hand reaches and finds mine. "It's the exact opposite. But it's really the same. My letting my body go, I choose myself over you all. It's really what we all have to do — choose ourselves. But we can't help feeling our dreadful inadequacy to others as we choose ourselves. The dreadful inadequacy of our choice." She shakes her head.

I think of my father's rumpled shirt, his uncombed hair. "Dad feels it too," I whisper.

"I know that. I know that," my mother says. Her sweater rises, fails. She cries soundlessly.

We fall quiet watching the light tilt from the sky, the purple shadows glide in like kites catching a down draft from the mountains. Tatters of maple leaves stick to Toby's sweater. A raggedy, patchwork scarecrow, he twists and twirls in the wind. The wind brushes up the leaves with an invisible, animistic broom. They spin like children, dizzying themselves until they drop. Even the stones grow souls this time of year.

"Wouldn't it be wonderful to be like that?" Mom asks me nodding at Toby. "He's like a puppy at play.   No self-consciousness."

"Or all self-consciousness," I say.

My mother glances at me, a fleeting but penetrating look, familiar to me since before I can remember, when I first looked at her face and she looked back at me with this meaning: I know you. I have always known you.

God forgive me, but how will I ever know myself without her regard?

Memories open themselves to me. I remember my father giving me a geography lesson at the kitchen table, stabbing the map with a pencil: we live here, he said, in this section of the Appalachian range. Our meadow was probably once ocean floor, accumulating layers of sediment until two continents collided and the momentum folded up the land as if it were a dinner napkin. But I did not believe him, did not believe that anything so stable, so immutable, so ageless could fold. But now I know it's true. I know that rocks grow restless, that mountains move.

The screen door slaps. My father, shirttail flapping, stands on the porch looking down on us. He sniffs the air suspiciously, or perhaps he is only breathing in the sad, perfect smell of apples rotting and, from somewhere far away, the smoke of red leaves burning. He spots Toby in the leaf pile and lopes over to him. Wordlessly he buries him in armful after armful of golden leaves. Toby laughs.

····

————————— **WITHOUT** —————————
A
GOODBYE

SLIPPING INTO STONE

Faye Moskowitz

My mother wrote me one letter in her life. She was in California then, seeking treatment for the disease whose name she was never allowed to utter, as if in some magical way, speaking the illness would confirm it. I found the letter in a dresser drawer the other day, written in the round hand of Americanization school on tissue-thin paper banded at the top with the narrow red edge of gum rubber where it was once attached to a tablet.

March 7, 1947
Dear Faye Chaim and Roger,
How are your kids? I am filling a little better. My beck still hurts. Today I was at doctors for a light treatment and Saturday I am going again for a tritement. I hope to god I shut fill better. Please write to me. How is evrething in the house? How does daddy fill. The weather is her wondufull nice and hot. I was sitting outside today. Well I have to say good night. I have to be in bet 9 o'clock for my health Take care of daddy.
your mother
Regart from evrywone.

On the back flap of the envelope, she had written her name, Sophie Stollman, and the street address of the sister with whom she was staying in Los Angeles. On the first line she had lettered in *Detroit, Mich:*, her home. Now, older than she was when she died, I am shattered by that confused address. Loneliness, homesickness and fear spill out of those laboriously penciled words, and the poignant error that was not a mistake, speaks to me still.

I suppose I realized from the beginning that my mother's illness was a serious one: I had seen the fearful loss of symmetry where the breast had been, the clumsy stitching around it, like that of a child sewing a doll's dress. I had caught her one morning weeping in front of the mirror as she poked at the rubber pad that kept working its way up to the open collar of her blouse. But I was sixteen years old and worried enough about keeping my own physical balance. One false step and I might fall off the edge of the world. I was afraid to walk the outer limits of her sickness. I dealt with death the way the rest of my family did . . . by denying it.

I buried myself in books, played the "will-he, won't-he" game of adolescence, worried about the atomic bomb, tried to keep my little brothers from acting like children in a house where the sounds of childhood were no longer appropriate. My father and I clung to each other, but the veil of my mother's illness fell between us, too, and we were silent.

She got worse, and the family began to gather. Covered dishes and pots of food appeared, crammed our refrigerator, molded, were thrown out and replaced by still more food. Visitors came and went, swirling like snowflakes in the downstairs rooms, sitting around the kitchen table drinking tea from glasses, talking, talking. Still, they said nothing, and it seemed to me, at times, their silence would awaken the dead.

A time came when my mother's wardrobe was reduced to open-backed hospital gowns. Our home was invaded twenty-four hours a day by a succession of starched uniforms and the incessant whisper of white nylon stockings. My mother was terrified by hospitals and refused to go, but still we were forced to trust her to the hands of strangers. She lay, as in a crib, imprisoned by iron bars; her own bed, where she had slept, knees in my father's back so many years, had been taken down to make room for a mattress scarcely wider than a coffin.

Alone for a moment, she called to me one day as I tiptoed past her bedroom. (Perhaps the nurse was downstairs preparing the unfamiliar food on which they kept her alive.) I stood next to her, watched her pluck at a fold in the bedclothes, smooth them, try to make the question casual by the homely gestures. "Faygele," she said, finally, "do you think I will ever get better?"

How could I answer her truthfully, being bound as inextricably as she was by the rules of the complicated deception we were playing out? Perhaps I understood in my heart's core that she was doomed. But I hadn't the permission of knowledge; I could only answer, "of course, of course," and help to wrap her more tightly alone inside her fear. She never asked me that question again.

A few weeks before my mother died, when the sounds coming from her room began to move beyond speech, an older cousin was given the responsibility of articulating to me the name of her disease. I remember he took me to an Italian restaurant where we stirred the food around on our plates, and to a movie afterward.

Cordoned off by heavy, velvet ropes, we stood in line under the prisms of rococo chandeliers, and there, surrounded by people I had never seen before, I was told the truth, at last. No room to cry in that glittering lobby, fire spurting from crystal lamps and mica-sparked placards. So I sat, in the darkness of the theater, watching *Johnny Belinda* flickering on the screen, the salt of buttered popcorn swallowed with the bitter salt of tears.

I was out late with friends the night of my mother's death. Walking alone up the darkened street, I saw my house, windows blazing as if for a party, and I knew what had happened. Word must have already spread, for on the sidewalk behind me I heard low voices and soft footsteps, stripped of purpose now, by her surrender.

In my mother's room, the mirrors, according to the old custom, had been shrouded (so the mourners would not have to confront their grief, some say) and damp, chill February fluttered curtains at the open window. My uncle, in a heavy jacket, sat next to his sister's bed. He would watch her until morning. "No, I'm not afraid," I told him. "Let me sit with her a little while."

She lay, hair bound in a white cloth, and I could feel her body, blood and bone under the sheet, pulling away from me, slipping into stone. The memories crowded around me, witnesses to my guilt: the many times I had resented caring for her, the times I had yearned to flee my house when her pain became an intimation of my own mortality.

I remembered, in the bas-relief of shame, the evening I came home from somewhere, to find her leaning on the kitchen sink, washing a stack of dishes I had left undone. "Shut up!" I had shouted when she spoke to me, angered at the robe and slippers, the cane lying on the floor, the medicine bottles, accouterments of a mother too sick to care for her own. Now we were cut off in mid-sentence. Now I would never be able to tell her how sorry I was for everything.

I still grieve for the words unsaid. Something terrible happens when we stop the mouths of the dying before they are dead. A silence grows up between us then, more profound than the grave. If we force the dying to go speechless, the stone dropped into the well will fall forever before the answering splash is heard.

PAPER, ROCK, SCISSORS

Lu Vickers

Mama loved to fish, but she couldn't swim. Not that that had anything to do with how many bream she caught, but I was a nine year old Girl Scout who had earned a swimming badge before I was eight, and it struck me as odd. In the long hot summers after my father died, she'd drag me out to Lake Mystic every day the sun shone.

"Either come with me or I'll take you to McPherson's."

Old Lady McPherson had a yard full of runny-nosed kids she took pay to keep. Mama knew I hated going there; it would mean I didn't belong anyplace else, so as much as I hated fishing, I would go with her. We'd drive out to Lake Mystic in our two-toned Fairlane, three or four cane poles poking out the back window vibrating in the wind like insect antennae, because Mama liked to drive fast. She said it made her feel like she was going somewhere. When we came around the curve to Bogie's Bait Shop, Mama would slow down and coast into the red dirt lot, the Fairlane creaking to a halt in the shade of a pecan tree.

We had to have the necessities, corks or lead weights or line or hooks: we always had to have three or four cans of Nu-Grape and Orange Crush. Bogie's had it all — a damp dirt floor, huge sweating coolers of ice-cold drinks, big concrete vats of minnows and huge wooden boxes filled with crickets or wigglers. When I opened the ragged screen door and stepped inside, I felt like I was in a cave. I liked leaning over the cool pools of bubbly water looking at the little minnows while Bogie counted out crickets for Mama.

After she stocked up on bait, we'd head on out to Lake Mystic, the Fairlane filled with the chirping sounds of the cricket box. I'll never forget the smell of that blue cardboard box with its little screen window and the little turds all over the bottom. But the crickets never dooked on me, just peed — right before I plunged the fish hook into their soft brown bellies.

Mama taught me how to hold them just right and I did or else they'd kick me with their spindly straw-like legs and I'd end up letting them crawl all over the rocks.

But my setting the crickets free didn't stop Mama. Every day it was "to the Lake or to McPherson's." Looking back on it now, I can see that I was babysitting her. She thought having me around would keep her from drowning.

My father died when I was two years old — he drove his cream colored '57 Buick off Victory Bridge and into the Flint River — so I never really knew him. But she loved him terribly. Used to, when she'd sit me on her knees to tell me stories, clasping my tiny hands in her big ones, she'd lean her face in close to mine till our noses touched. Then she'd stare deep into my eyes and whisper, "You've got your daddy's sky-blue eyes."

People in Faceville said she wasn't the same after he died, but she was always the same to me. She cried a lot and begged me to help her — to do what, I never knew. In September of '65, the day I was supposed to start the first grade, I was getting dressed and a button popped off my blouse and clicked across the wooden bedroom floor. Mama got down on her knees and picked it up, holding it in her fingers as if it were alive and had popped off my blouse on purpose to make me late. Her hands shook so bad she couldn't hold the needle and thread to sew it back on, so she started crying and laid on my bed, covering her face with a corner of the patchwork quilt she'd made.

I stood beside her unsure of what to do, but I knew not to cry. I rubbed her back and hugged her and finally she got up, dried her tears and called the school and calmly told the secretary I wasn't coming that day. Instead, she took me to a wide open field and we flew kites against the warm wind.

"Your father loved kites," she told me, pulling the string toward her, the kite rising higher against the wind.

"He could make a kite out of just about anything — a grocery bag and a couple of sticks strung together with butcher's string. That man loved the wind."

She showed me how to loop the kites through the air like big dizzy butterflies, and when they flew so high we could barely see them, we turned the strings loose and the kites disappeared into the whiteness of the sky as if we'd never held them. Mama drove us back home, the Fairlane fishtailing from ditch to ditch, kicking up dirt like an angry dog.

She sent me to school the next day.

Somehow we made it. She saw to it that I did all the things a kid's supposed to do and at the end of the year she sent me to school with a small watercolor she painted for my first grade teacher — a tiny hummingbird hovering over a large red flower.

Sundays she dressed me up in flower print dresses and took me to the First Baptist Church down on Washington Street. Polyestered ladies with beehive hairdos would come up to Mama and mew about what a good job she was doing with me and how pretty and well-behaved I was, and I would duck behind her legs embarrassed by my perfection.

When I was about ten or so, she made me join the church choir. Even though I hated singing, I would go because I thought it would make her happy. When the pianist began playing *Bringing in the Sheaves* or *Standing on the Promises*, my mind would wander back to Mama off alone somewhere. I could just imagine her going back home to sit on the porch and rock, tears rolling down her cheeks, and before I knew it Tammy Kincaid would be giggling and poking me in the ribs. I'd start humming instead of singing the words, like an old woman lost in her thoughts. Once, after Mama dropped me off at the church, she came right back looking for me, and when she came into the room where we were practicing, I froze.

She quietly told the choir director she needed me and I relaxed a little. As soon as I stepped out of the group of children and got her out of the room where I could breathe normally, she started crying about why did my father have to die, as if I had caused his death.

She drove me out to the cemetery where he was buried, stopping along the way to pick wildflowers out of ditches: black-eyed susans, violets, buttercups. She laid them on the blue vinyl front seat of the Fairlane and when we got out to the cemetery we carried them over and she laid them on his grave.

Lying in the grass, leaning against the headstone, she told me stories I'd heard a number of times — how he used to bring her daisies and how he'd once flown an airplane so low over her daddy's house that he nearly clipped the tops off the pine trees.

[77]

She talked herself all the way through their courtship to my conception: she talked till her voice became a whisper and the sun set and then we drove home quietly. I held my head out the window letting the cool night air wash over me, hoping the world would be different by the time we got home. We drove up to the house and she went straight in to bed, closing the door behind her and I sat on the porch reading *The Bobbsey Twins*.

Most days, I got up, got dressed, and went to school without waking her. For a long time I would avoid stepping on cracks in the sidewalk, not because I believed that childish rhyme about breaking your mother's back, but because I hoped my persistence would somehow make a difference.

It didn't. Mama tended her sadness like a gardener tending her plants. All I could ever be sure of was nothing.

Once, when I was about thirteen, I was playing with my favorite toy, a plastic guitar with Elvis Presley's picture on it. I was pretending to be Elvis, gyrating wildly about the dining room, singing *You ain't nothin' but a hound dog*. Mama came flying out of her bedroom as if it'd caught on fire, snatched the guitar out of my hands, smashed it on the floor, strings twanging; then she stomped Elvis' broken plastic face to bits with her bedroom shoes. She didn't even say she was sorry. I walked out of the house and down the road, wondering what life would be like if I ran away. I could hop on a boxcar and ride down to Bristol and pick peas for a living.

As I grew older, I became less and less like a daughter. When I was about sixteen, I would be sitting in the dining room in the dark watching *Evening at Pops* with Arthur Fiedler. I'd hear the scrape of a window being raised and I'd take a deep breath and my heart would beat fast and I'd wish I was one of those dressed-up ladies in the audience on TV watching Arthur conduct for real.

Mama would crawl out of the window on the front of the house as if she were crawling out of the eye on the head of some large decaying animal. Then she'd sit in the azalea bushes on her haunches with her arms wrapped around her knees as if she were some sort of wildlife herself.

I'd go out to get her. By now I didn't worry about the neighbors. It was dark anyway. "Mama, please come back into the house. Please. You're behaving like a child. You're scaring me."

She would look up at me, her coal black eyes glittering in the moonlight. She wouldn't move so I would sit out there with her, hunched over in the damp grass, the smell of earth rising between us, lightning bugs twinkling in the distance. Finally, I would grow tired and go back into the house, which glowed with the strange blue light on the television. I'd turn it off and climb into bed and stare out at the darkness, trying to see the particles of color which compose the night.

I spent a lot of nights that way, unable to sleep, wondering what would happen. The older I got, the more I talked to her. The only solutions I could think of were simple ones. "Paint more. Write it down. Go to a psychiatrist. Find someone to love." I followed her around in the twilight after sundown, as she dragged the hose around the yard watering the grass and I told her my dreams, and when that didn't work, jokes. She would smile awhile, then shut the water off, coil the hose up and say, "I wish I could crawl under that blanket of grass and go to sleep."

When I go to sleep now, I dream of her smiling in photographs. Standing there looking beautiful, because she was. She had perfect teeth and dark smooth skin and wavy brown hair which she always wore loose.

In the photograph of my dream, she stood on the grassy bank in the breeze which blew off the Flint River. Her eyes had a soft look to them and she seemed to be whispering something. I wished I could hire someone to read her lips, so much did it seem like she was saying something.

I was never any good at reading people's lips, although I have heard your mind would do it naturally if you let it. I never could. It was as if the wind caught her voice like a kite and shot it up in the air out of my reach. I only sensed it was important from the way her face looked.

One day she told me she was going to do it, but I couldn't hear her. She said, "Sara, I want to be cremated when I die. I want you to sprinkle my ashes into the river. It'll give the fish a thrill."

Okay, Ma, sure. In fifty years. The next day when I woke,

the house was still and quiet, the usual morning smells of coffee and toast strangely missing. The house felt empty. Even before I walked down the hall to her bedroom, I knew she was gone. All I had left was an image of her waving goodbye and saying words I couldn't understand.

FORGOTTEN SORROW

Susan Christian

I don't call my mother Mother. I call her Betty. Betty, my father's first wife. Betty, my aunts' sister. Betty, my grandmother's daughter.

My only memory of Betty is suspect. I am in a crib in a dark room. The door cracks open. I see my mother's silhouette against the distant slit of light. I see her smile at me and at life in general. All's well.

But I would have been too young, most likely, to remember such an encounter. Perhaps the woman at the door was my Aunt Judy. Perhaps I have turned the image into Betty for some link beyond home movies and borrowed recollections.

In the home movie, it is my first birthday. I plop my hand in the cake as Betty watches, amused. Vying for the spotlight, my sister Elizabeth hammily skips in front of the camera. Betty swoops me up and with graceful deftness simultaneously bounces her one year old, humors her three year old, slices the cake.

She has not yet learned that the bothersome ache in her leg is bone cancer. She will be gone a few months before my second birthday, a few weeks after her thirty-first birthday.

Now, thirty-two years later, I am two years older than my mother — her youth stalled in an eternal freeze-frame.

From the home movies, I know that Betty was brunette, petite, wholesomely pretty — high cheekbones, pug nose, sweet smile. From the borrowed recollections, I know that she was gentle and refined.

I know almost nothing about her final days. My paternal grandmother once told me that Betty put on lipstick minutes before dying; she wanted to look nice for her husband. Such glimpses of that wrenching time have been rare — thankfully rare, so I've thought.

When a young widower reweds, a conspiracy of silence (both unintentional and good-intentioned) prevails for the sake of the new marriage. The father does not speak of his first wife in front of his second wife; there are feelings to consider. The grandmother does not regale her grandchildren with anecdotes about her daughter; they have another mother now.

"Your mother died when you were a baby? That must have been hard for you," I have heard throughout my life.

"No, I don't remember any of it," I denied, routinely and sincerely — as if pain not remembered is pain not important.

On the occasions that I allowed myself to mourn, I focused my sorrow on Dad, the one who remembers. Seeing *Love Story* as a teen, I cried from a deep and unrecognized source, my father's tragedy personified. But I never reserved a tear for Elizabeth, nor for myself.

Yet over the past year, as I watch my niece, Alex, sprout to the age I was when I was being shuttled from aunt to aunt by my devastated father, and as I observe the mother-child bond so crucial to a toddler's sense of security, I find myself yearning for Betty in a way that never before dawned on me.

Alex knows what's going on. She spots a storybook picture of papa bear falling on his head and bursts into sobs, fretting, "Daddy hurt!" She catches my sister dressing for work and demands, "Don't do that."

A long-buried truth stabs at me: I, too, knew what was going on. I knew that my mother lost the strength to play with me, then I knew that she vanished. I knew that my caretakers were sad and distracted. I knew that my grandmother wept as she changed my diaper, that Dad's voice cracked when he read to me, that Aunt Myra's smile quivered. Although I would not remember those things, I always would know them.

Suddenly, I grieve Betty's death as if I could, in fact, remember it. For the first time, I pity myself at eighteen months and my sister at three years. I pity my father and my grandmothers, aunts and uncles rolled back in time to 1957.

Most of all, I empathize with Betty, I can imagine — I want to imagine — what she endured.

"If I had to say goodbye to Alex like Betty had to say goodbye to us..." my sister reflected, the idea too overwhelming for completion.

She remembers it: the ambulance attendants carrying Betty away on a stretcher. "Dad said, 'Come tell your mother goodbye, honey,'" Elizabeth recalled. "I was jumping up and down on the couch, and I said, 'Look, Mommy, I can almost touch the ceiling.' I wanted to make her proud of me. She said, 'You're such a big girl.'"

Odd. Elizabeth had never before shared this memory with me. She, also, had taken part in the conspiracy of silence — as had I, choosing not to feel the wounds that others chose not to expose.

The survivors survived. Two years after Betty's death, Dad married a woman who rightfully would claim possession of the title Mom. My four delightful brothers came.

Dad earned himself an admirable life, full of devoted friends and great achievement. Still, I cannot help but notice his aura of stoicism.

Elizabeth and I enjoy rewarding careers, and we've always been popular and adventuresome. Still, I cannot help but wonder how different I might be if I'd had my mother. Would I be so rootless? Would I have left my hometown, Austin, for Los Angeles? Or would I have settled down in Texas as my cousins did? Would I appreciate what I have rather than want what I can't have? Would I trust commitments to last?

My sister gives me one more scrap of our dying mother: Elizabeth is in the bathtub; Betty, wearing a nightgown, supervises from the lidded commode. "You missed a spot of soap," she says, then leans over to assist, but stops in mid-motion. "I can't do it for you, honey, but I can show you how," Betty offers instead.

As I listened to this, a slap of anger grazed me. "Get up and bathe your child!" I thought, absurdly, shamefully annoyed at Betty for letting herself fail us. My silent outburst felt so new and bizarre that I could not admit it to my sister.

I exaggerated when I said that. I want to know what my mother endured. In some ways I regret gaining possession of those two vignettes: Betty on the stretcher, Betty by the bathtub. Each stings with the sharpness of a raw gash. Someday they will blend into the picture of my total experience; for now they jut out like unruly misfits.

This overdue mourning has not been easy; still, I cannot help but think that it is necessary.

COLLECTING PIECES

Sue Rochman

I

Once, ritual lament would have been chanted;
women would have been paid to beat their breasts
and howl for you all night, when all is silent.
Where can we find such customs now?
— Rainer Maria Rilke, *Requiem for a Friend*

October 4, 1977, Dear diary, It's 4:40 and I just found out Mom died at 4:00. Oh my God! These are the words I find when I look into my old journal, the words of my fifteen year old self. Tucked in between journal entries on friends, shopping and popularity, these words stand alone, artifacts of my pain.

No one had taught me how to speak about death. When I tried, speech lodged in my throat. Like a child, I stumbled over fragments of words. Once uttered, the sounds were wrong, harsh, staining the silence reverberating around me. My mother's name became a hushed whisper on my family's lips. Their silence captured me and my own grew quickly. Close-tongued, I joined with the others in building a house of silence — rooms where thoughts could not grow and emotions ran dry. As a teenager, it was easier to contemplate what I would wear the next day, the problems with my hair, or if I was popular, than to begin to understand the staid silence or comprehend what my life would now be. I did not want to think about what I could no longer say. "Mom, come here! I want to show you something," or "What was it like when . . . " were now only echoes of my past. Feeling this, knowing this, would mean having to admit that a part of myself would no longer flourish. Cut off near the root, at fifteen, parts of my life just stopped. In many ways, I had died too.

II

We transform these Things;
they aren't real, they are only the reflections
upon the polished surface of our being.

On my desk a lavender, flowered tin box sits amidst scattered papers, earrings, an open book. Inside, one atop the other, lay pictures of my mother. Over the past twelve years I have secretly taken these pictures from other family albums. Concealed in my coat pockets, suitcases, purses, I have taken these photographs from my father's house. My need — to make these static images into memory. I examine these pictures regularly. They nourish the grief which edges my life. I touch my finger to the smooth, glossy surface. Shades of white, gray and black, I wish to infuse them with my touch, my heat, my life; color them with love, make them speak.

Over and over I pick up these photographs. The hardest part are the questions I cannot ask her, the answers I will never know. I stare at her eyes, trying to look into them. Soon I am shaking these photographs in my frustration. What were you thinking? What did you want? What did you believe?

If I put these photographs in some semblance of order I can chronicle parts of my mother's life: her childhood, marriage to my father, my birth, our family life, the beginning of the cancer. Only recently have I noticed something new: the pictures of my mother as a child have writing on the back in pen and in pencil. In pen are the additions my grandmother must have added after I was born. On some, she has noted similarities between my mother and myself. I am interested, intrigued, jealous. This link between mother and daughter is an experience I will never know.

I look through these photographs thinking of my grandmother, my mother, myself. The date on the photograph: September 1938. My mother sits on my grandfather's shoulders. *Me and my Daddy dear* in my grandmother's scrawl graces the back. Another, November 1939: my mother at three, feeding her doll. My grandmother had penned, *Remember your rocker? You practiced then giving a bottle. Now, God bless you, it's for real.*

I think of my grandmother, a woman haunted by her inability to raise my mother. My mother had been raised in a home for children; mentally unstable, my grandmother could not maintain a household. The role of mother evaded her; her mind and body betrayed her. She could not be the provider when my mother was a child, nor could she be the protector and harbor her daughter from disease. There is an eeriness in my grandmother's words. They are the coded messages of a love oft interrupted, a claim to what should have been hers.

Interspersed in my box with pictures of my mother as a child are pictures of myself. My childhood photographs mirror my mother's. Similar features, similar hair, in some I could be her, she me. When she was alive, family members and friends would frequently comment on how much I looked like her. Now, no one ever does. Yet, I hear the unspoken voices in the silence that follows me; I know: I am a constant reminder to others. As the years go by my own silence grows, louder and louder it ripens within me. If we cannot speak of her existence, how can I give life to mine?

The earliest picture that I have of myself: eyes wide open, wrapped in a pink blanket, held to my mother's breast. My mother is gazing down at me, only the side of her face in view — if I could see her eyes, what would they tell me? Her hand, resting on top of my small body, covers it from side to side. Inscribed on the back of the photograph is my mother's distinct, flowing script: *Aug. 31, 1962, 3 days old.* How I hunger for writing by my mother. Upon turning eighteen I had hoped my father would say to me, "Here these are for you," and hand me the words my mother had left me — a journal, letters, her wishes for me. Hollywood movies tainting my life, creating expectations. Only recently have I stopped imagining that one day I could be looking through old boxes and crates and come across these messages I had yearned for.

Dead at forty-two, motherhood eluded my mother as well. Leaving behind three children, fifteen, thirteen and ten, her fears reverberate in my own life. She was afraid of the cancer growing silently within her embattled body scarred and disfigured by chemotheraphy, radiation, the surgeon's tools. But she would not relinquish herself to death, admit its possibility to her children, or perhaps even to herself. Her last week alive she was in the hospital, barely able to sit up, stay awake, swallow water. My sisters and I were brought daily to visit. But what does it mean when a parent lies. When death's reality is shaded. When the last words before "I love you," are: "When I come home . . . . " She refused to let go, so how could I?

I can't imagine my own life past forty-two. I don't know how I will look as I age. I don't know how I'll grow old. Part of me fears that I am too similar; that one day my body will also turn against me, that like my mother and grandmother, motherhood will elude me as well. My journals are a legacy. Numbered in my 'save' boxes, these writings await the daughter I hope to have. I don't want for her to have to guess, to make up stories, to covet tattered photos. I elicit a promise from my lover: tell her all the silly stories, that I was fun and wild and crazy. Make her feel how I lived.

III

We need, in love, to practice only this:
Letting each other go. For holding on
comes easily; we do not need to learn it.

It is the present. My mother is still alive. We are still arguing. The tension remains. The wanting to be close, the pulling away, the wanting to reach out. Yet I will not allow closeness. I move toward a desk, her desk. Framed photographs sit on top: images of my father, my grandfather, my sisters, myself.

My dream pushes me from sleep, I awaken with memory's tears. My private picture show follows me, haunts me. Awake or asleep I cannot forget; the questioning, searching eyes: my mother's pained face.

My life is consumed by the insistence of memory. I acquiesce to the driving force of my emotions. It is many years later and still I struggle for release — from the guilt, from the sorrow, from the silence. Haltingly, cautiously, I try to speak to others. Outlining the silence, my words give shape to near-forgotten memories. The silhouette of my grief slowly begins to take form.

A friend shares a story with me about saying goodbye to

those we have lost. The story is of a woman and the handful of balloons she brought to the grave of her husband. At the cemetery, as voices joined in prayer, the balloons were released. The purpose: to allow the soul of the dead to move on, unbind memories, free the living.

That night I dream:

I am holding five white balloons, they float above me, their long strings held tight by my hand. The last orange-pink tones of the sun's colors are fading; it is time to let go. But I am incapable of untangling the memories. I cannot let go. In my dream I begin to rise with the balloons, ensnared by memory's unraveling threads. "Hold on," I call, "take me with you." But my weight is an anchor. I am jumping, running, my hands raised in the air. I try to let go, the strings waver in front of me, hampering my steps, surrounding my ankles. Flung to the ground, my fingers claw the damp earth. I cannot move. Five round white circles float above me.

IV

The dead have their own tasks
But help me, if you can without distraction,
as what is farthest sometimes helps: in me.

It was eleven years after my mother died before I returned to the cemetery to see her grave. It was a chilly, California, January day. Even though the cemetery was only thirty minutes from our family's house, we had never gone. I didn't remember exactly where she was buried. As I drove into the grounds, memories emerged, revived by the buildings, statues, hills. I was given a number and a map. Embarrassed that I didn't know where her grave was, I walked up and down the hillside, until finally I found her name. I looked, then looked away, took a deep breath and knelt down. Slowly my fingers stroked each letter of her name. A decade of tears stained the bronzed marker. I sat down by her side.

In July I again returned. My lover took a picture of the marker. I couldn't take it myself. But I needed the photograph. Another stolen image to lay alongside the others. The collected pieces of our past. It is how I grapple with the pain. It is how I tell her I'm sorry. It is how we will both let go.

THE EDITH PAPERS

Arupa Chiarini

I got a note in the mail a few days ago. It said, *Edith Rogers' funeral was March 29 in San Antonio. I thought you might not have heard.* The note writer, an old friend of my grandmother's, was right. I did not know whether my mother was dead or alive. I lived with her for the first three years of my life, and for one troubled summer when I was eighteen. When I was five she visited me in Vermont and I begged her to take me with her when she left. She said to me, "I'm sorry. I have to live my own life."

When I was thirty-five, I wrote a poem to my mother, a poem of love and forgiveness. I got her number and called her, wanting to read her this poem. She cut me short, offended that I felt I had anything to forgive her for. She said, "You were cruel, selfish, and manipulative from the day you were born."

She was fifty-four then. She had gone on to lead her own life, which included a new marriage and two more children. She raised these two children. My sister Susan and I had neither mother nor father. We did not even have each other. My grandmother was harsh and abusive. Susan's foster-caretakers did not allow her to visit me, ever. She lived five miles away from me and I never saw her. I don't know where she is or how her life turned out.

In spite of all this, I have to take time out to grieve for my mother. I did not have a substitute mother to give that love to. The love I would have given my mother lies in my chest like a great, heavy stone. If I had known she was dying, I would have flown to San Antonio to see her one last time.

I am struggling to do my grieving without goodbyes, ceremonies, a church service, or acknowledgement that I ever had a mother or that that mother's death would mean anything to me. There are socially prescribed rituals for death, dying and mourning, but they don't apply to me.

I am a romantic and a reader of books. It was not supposed to happen this way. My mother, when death approached, was supposed to send for me. We were supposed to reconcile our long war. She was supposed to say, "I'm sorry I couldn't raise you. I was only nineteen and I had a lot of problems." I was supposed to say, with tears raining down my face, "I understand. I'm sorry I never understood before." But I was the child who did not exist, the family member who did not exist.

I called my half-brother to find out how she died. He told me, briefly. I strained to hear him say that she mentioned me, at the end acknowledged my existence. But he did not, and I could not bear to ask. I assume she told him bad things about me, made me out to be beyond redemption.

He told me that he and my half-sister, Dawn, feel very bad that she died, and I am glad that she was loved at the end. I want to take the stone out of my chest and give it to someone. I am thinking about my memorial for her, a tree I will plant somewhere, sometime, something I will do to stand testimony that I had a mother and that that mother died. She is no longer around to tear it up.

I wake up on my mother's twelfth morning of being dead and think, "This cannot go on." I cannot go on measuring time in this way. Did I really believe so deeply that we would one day become friends? I have taken off three days from work to mourn her. I want my allotted days of mourning. Today there is a heavy rain falling. I realize I have energy this morning. Yesterday morning I had none. It is Wednesday and usually I would go to two cleaning jobs. But it is one of my days of mourning, and the day stretches ahead of me, full of possibilities.

Ezra will go off to school, and Bob will go over to Sudheer's house to work on his computer. I will be alone in this house on a rainy day. I have always loved rainy days. To me, falling rain is like some kind of truce from God. "The sun will not beat down on you today. You can stay in the house and be cozy. You can make cocoa and listen to the radio."

I am remembering now to be grateful for my pain. It is some sort of gift. Gratitude brings a dimension of light to what was a dark and dreadful cancer eating away in the depths of myself. I am one with all those who have ever suffered pain. I am learning something new — that it is necessary to be grateful for pain in order to learn anything from it.

I lie in bed at night and sort through my memories of Edith, which begin with a dim flash of being in a baby swing in the kitchen of an apartment somewhere on the East coast. I search in vain for one memory of Edith smiling at me or hugging me. Instead I remember Edith hitting me, Edith's tongue stinging me, standing before her mute, unable to defend myself. She is angry because I am cold, she is angry because I need to pee, she is angry because I accidentally disclosed some secret to my grandmother. "I see that I will never be able to tell you anything," she says to me, her voice cold with scorn that causes my very soul to shiver. I am seven and I don't know why I am so bad, so unworthy. She is magical to me. Tall and beautiful with shining black hair and smooth, olive skin and dark, mysterious eyes. To be loved by someone so beautiful would be the most wonderful thing in the world. But she does not love me, she will not love me, I am inadequate, I am simply not good enough. I am so very, very bad that she will not allow me to live with her. My friends all live with their mothers. To be so bad that one is not allowed to live with one's mother is the greatest curse imaginable. There is a gulf between me and other human beings, a gulf of evil and darkness and shame.

Even now, my friends cannot relate to what I am experiencing. They know my mother died, but how strange that there was no final visit, that I heard of her death in a note in the mail, three days after she was buried. They cannot imagine such a thing. What did I do that I was barred from her final illness? There is no answer to that. I carry my pain in a basket and offer it to God, who may be the only one who understands it. The only one who knows where it came from, and who I am and who she was.

Edith was my link to magic. I spent hours sitting on the front steps of my grandmother's house watching cars drive by. Although I never said it aloud, I was waiting for Edith to come home. When I was eight she disappeared, moved West with some guy named Robert Rogers, and we did not hear from her for three years. I would not see her again until I was seventeen. Maybe if she had looked like me, short and chubby with hair that turned into frizz on rainy days, she would never have left me. But Edith was exotic, a Spanish beauty, tall and slender with black hair and brown eyes and a velvet-smooth voice with a hint of a southern accent. She was fearless. She would walk into my grandmother's kitchen and scoop fried potatoes right out of the pan — and get away with it. She had traveled. She drove cars and changed jobs and had boyfriends. She laughed out loud and made jokes about sex. My grandmother, a frugal and ferocious puritan, seemed afraid of her.

My grandmother did not want to raise another child and talked endlessly about "making Edith take you back." Nothing ever came of it. Edith did not want me back, and she moved through the world like an exotic bird who could not be trapped into any cage not of her own choosing. I thought that if only I could become linked with her, I too would have magic.

During the summer of my eighteenth birthday, I lived with Edith. She rode me endlessly about my appearance. I was fat and awkward. I had pimples and my hair frizzed gracelessly around my face. She was ashamed to be seen with me. She told me I needed a new wardrobe. We drove all over Oklahoma City putting beautiful new outfits into layaway at little dress shops where she was on a first-name basis with the clerks. She had me pay the layaway fees, promising that she would keep up the subsequent payments. She never did. I lost my layaway fees and never got any of the beautiful new clothes. When I protested, she shrugged it off, reminding me that I had been eating her food all summer and shouldn't complain.

The next summer, after my first year of college, I wanted to go back to my grandmother in Vermont. I wrote to her telling her when I would arrive. My grandmother never replied. Instead, I got a letter from Edith saying, *Your grandmother cannot afford to keep you. The grocery bill went down by eleven dollars a month after you left. You must find your own accommodations.* Those words burned inside me like a malignant growth for the rest of my life. They translated out to: *Eleven dollars a month is more than you are worth.* I did not go home. Instead I had a nervous breakdown. I worked at a library for $1.05 an hour and lived at a boardinghouse that offered kitchen privileges.

Every moment I was not at the library I spent playing solitaire, obsessively, hour after hour, until four and five in the morning. I could not eat or sleep. I went to a doctor who put me on Thorazine. The Thorazine attacked my liver and I ended up in the hospital for two weeks. Edith called up and screamed at me in rage, because the hospital sent the bill to her.

I went off into the darkness, into many years of depression, anxiety, phobias, substance abuse, destructive relationships — and all along Edith glittered at the edges of my consciousness — beautiful, thin, exotic, self-assured.

I know that she too was a victim of child abuse, and that she died prematurely after a troubled life. I am profoundly glad that she was able to make friends and to raise two of her four children — and so to be loved and mourned at the end. But still I explore the Edith that I knew. I have been diagnosed as having post-traumatic stress syndrome, the Viet Nam vet's disease. I understand that now as a fancy name for having no one to talk to. The ordinary traumas of life, breaking a leg or having one's house burn down, get talked out. Each listener offers sympathy, advice, or practical help. The story is told and retold until healing is complete. But there are some stories no one wants to hear about, or can't relate to if they do, and those stories stay inside, eating away at health and sanity, causing unbearable pressure. Even now I feel foolish saying that my grandmother attacked me with knives, that she regarded me as a vessel inhabited by Satan, that I was afraid to go to sleep at night because of her threats that she would murder me in my bed, that she screamed "pauper, pauper, pauper" at me while I ate my food. All of that is true, but no one wants to hear about it anymore than people want to hear about what happened in Viet Nam. The dark secrets I shared with Edith are beyond my conscious recall. I only know that whenever my mother touched me, my skin crawled. I was once forced by circumstance to share a bed with her, when I was twenty, and I lay awake all night, perched rigidly at the very edge of the bed. For me she was literally Mother Kali —the creator and the destroyer.

I grew up watching television shows like *Ozzie and Harriet, Leave it to Beaver,* and *Father Knows Best.* These shows had simple plots in which there was a Dark Moment when a child, either through fate, misjudgment, or some petty fault, found itself cast into outer darkness, unloved, doomed. Then, after the final commercial, the fault would be redeemed or the misunderstanding cleared up and the child would receive a shower of hugs, kisses, repeated assurances of what a wonderful child it was. It seemed to me like a version of April Fools'. A child is temporarily led to believe that it is an unloved, worthless creature. Then its parents and brothers and sisters jump out from behind the couch saying, "It was all a mistake. Of course we love you with all our hearts. Come to us so we can shower you with good things!" I've spent most of my life waiting for the denouement, waiting for my father and Edith and Susan to jump out from behind the couch wearing little paper hats and carrying presents. Then we will sit down and they will explain that it was all a terrible mistake, and now we are going to live happily ever after.

This is really what Edith's death means to me, or to some small, hidden part of myself — no paper hats, no presents, no hugs, no explanations, no Happy Ending. No ending at all, because Edith is dead, and my father and Susan are lost in the vast universe. I am sorry that Edith is dead because she loved being alive so much. Her animosity to me did not extend to life in general. She had an uproarious, infectious laugh. She loved good books, outrageous ideas, all-night poker games, and going out on the town. She once said to me, the summer I was eighteen, that most sickness is imaginary. She said, "You can feel sick and if someone came along and said, 'Hey, let's go dancing' you'd just forget you were sick and get up and go." She was fond of saying that the major piece of advice she could pass on to her children was, "Never bet on an inside straight."

Goodbye, Edith. I needed to talk about you, and how it felt having you as a mother. I'm sorry you didn't live longer. I'm sorry we never got anything straightened out. I always admired your chutzpah and your joie de vivre. I have spent my life learning how to live with your absence. In a way, I have learned as much from you as any daughter ever learned from her mother.

GRIEF POSTPONED

Judith Barrington

Instead of watching my mother grow old, or rushing to the hospital as she faced a major illness; instead of going to her house full of concern or resentment month after month, or holding her hand in some hospital bed with machines beeping and the family forced into closeness; instead of any one of the many versions of daughterly involvement I might have had with my mother's death, I watched it on television along with everyone else.

Some images I lived with were: a shaky aerial shot of a ship swathed in dense grey smoke; a hundred women in black, wailing in the street outside the Greek Shipping Line in St. James' London; my mother stepping down from the burning ship's deck onto the first rung of a ladder. I lived with these symbols for about twenty years before I really began to mourn.

It is difficult to feel connected to the event when your mother, who represents the closest and most intimate tie you have in the world, dies in an entirely public fashion, far away from home. It's hard to find a personal connection to the event. Or even really to believe it has happened. My mother and father both died on a cruise ship that caught fire: a Christmas cruise in 1963 when I was nineteen. For five days the ship, which was carrying more than a thousand passengers (most of whom would survive), was watched by the whole world, and particularly by the British public, since a majority of the passengers were from the United Kingdom.

This public aspect of my mother's dying was certainly not the only barrier to my grief, but it was a major one. One weekend she and my father were at home talking about the cruise they were about to go on, and a few days later I was reading a newstand headline at Piccadilly Circus: *Lakonia on*

Fire! When my mother's death began, she was already out of sight, out of my life. I had no connection to it except through the media.

It was very hard to believe she was actually dead. Her body and my father's were both picked up by one of the many rescue ships that hovered in the area, unable to get close enough to pick up survivors from the sea. Because men carry wallets, which makes them easier to identify, we heard about my father first. My brother had to fly to Gibraltar to identify my mother and he decided then and there, without consulting me, that our parents should be buried in Gibraltar. At the memorial service at our local church in Brighton, there were no coffins. The whole experience, in fact, was disembodied. I had to create my mother's death for myself.

My mother had always been terrified of the sea. She got seasick at the slightest provocation and hated to go on my father's sailboat. She had been known to walk out of a movie when the storm-at-sea scene came on. It was hard to accept that she had gone on this cruise at all, and harder to realize that she had only done it to please my father, who had wanted to go for years and had finally worn her down. But her fear of the sea provided ample material for my imagination, as I played out her last few days in my mind. I knew better than to picture her in a panic, yet a heroic stance was equally unlikely. I knew, from the evidence of their stopped watches, that she and my father had both gone into the sea at the same time, but I couldn't imagine how they had treated each other at that moment. Was he reassuring? Impatient? Did they break through to something real that I never knew existed between them?

Since I am a poet, one of the ways I tried to create a believable death for my mother was in my poems. I tried, year after year, to write about the accident, but was always afraid of the drama, always afraid of writing it as if it were an adventure story. What would have made the poems work, but what was missing for so long, were my feelings.

Most of my speculation about the event was focused on my mother. I paid little attention to my father, believing myself to be angry at him in death as I had been in life. But my mother was at the center of a public drama that I was turning into a private melodrama. I had no encouragement to think about myself, none of the kind of support that would have helped me feel entitled to all the fears and sorrows I was so skillfully repressing. My brother and sister were much older than I, with families of their own, and anyway we had never been close. They offered a place to stay whenever I needed and a sense of family, but they never shared their feelings, never talked about *it* with me.

Looking back on it, I sometimes think that a crucial block in my grieving process fell into place at the moment I learned of my father's death. The same moment I realized I was going to be left alone to cope.

We had been waiting day after day for news, as survivors in lifeboats were picked up by rescue ships and their names were added to the taped message that we called and listened to every hour. My sister and I were staying at my brother's house, where the three of us took turns making the call, day and night. It was my brother who made the call when my father's name had been added to the list. His body had been found by a British Navy ship.

I was standing by the window of the bedroom when my brother opened the door and said, "They've found father's body. He's dead." I was looking out the window and didn't turn around. I knew it meant my mother was dead too. There was a click as the door closed, and I thought my brother had come into the room and was walking across to me. After a while, when nothing happened, I turned around. The room was empty. The click had been the door shutting as he left.

Later, I realized that I ought to have feelings. People told me it was unhealthy not to be sad. But I couldn't do anything about it. I didn't cry at all for a year and I didn't menstruate for two. The one woman who tried to comfort me right after the accident ended up seducing me, thus offering me a quick escape into a sexual identity crisis, extreme guilt, and an even greater reason to hide my feelings. I began to obsess about sex and relationships, becoming addicted to intrigue, fast pseudo intimacy, and sexual intensity permeated with guilt, and for twenty years the addiction worked as addictions are supposed to: it kept away the pain.

Meanwhile, I was able to think and talk quite rationally about my mother's death, but underneath I felt guilty for not having been there — guilty that I hadn't done anything to save her. I fantasized rescuing her — doing the heroic thing to get her in a lifeboat; succeeding where my father had failed miserably. I also felt guilty about what I saw as the melodramatic story surrounding her death. I was extremely sensitive to drawing attention to myself — something my family had always effectively prohibited — and I thought people would think I was trying to get attention if I even mentioned the story; after all, it was quite an attention-getter. I both wanted, and didn't want, to be a tragic figure left behind in the wake of an international disaster. Mostly I would avoid telling people and then, later, would feel more guilt at their discomfort when they made a faux pas that they couldn't help because they didn't know. When I did tell them, I would throw it out brightly, then change the subject, giving no opportunity for anyone to pity me or be embarrassed.

Later I got myself into counseling and tackled the whole thing head on. But still, even then, I didn't understand that I had to focus on myself. I spent session after session speculating on my mother's experience: were there really sharks in the sea as some newspapers had suggested? Had she been furious at my father for getting her there? For missing out when the lifeboats left? Had she, in fact, refused to get into a lifeboat? Somehow I thought if I could just "know" how it had really happened, I could put it behind me.

When, finally, I began to feel my mother's loss, the images associated with her death were entirely worn out. Where once they might have triggered real feeling, now they seemed like scenes from a movie I had seen too many times. I couldn't think about her loss in terms of the burning ship or the crew wives wailing in the street. I had to think about it in terms of my own life and her absence from it.

For a whole year or more I walked around in acute pain. I felt silly suffering for something that had happened twenty years earlier, but I felt it anyway. After all those years of trying to get to it by way of the dark, oily ocean and the melting bulkheads, finally I came to the grief by a different route: I had no mother; I had had no mother for twenty years. It was as simple as that.

Now my images were ones of my own life, not of my

mother's horrifying experience. They involved an enormous absence in my life over some twenty years, an absence that I began to see stretching into the future too. I started to notice other women's relationships with their mothers, both good and bad, and wondered what mine with my mother would have been like had she lived. In my mind, I played out some of the issues that surely would have come up between us, the choices I had made in my life that she would have disapproved. How would she have taken my being a poet, a lesbian? I lived through those discussions without her and, later, allowed myself to feel her pride in my achievements, also without her. I thought about things we might have done together, visits she could have made to me in my new home, thousands of miles from hers. I started missing my mother in hundreds of tangible ways.

My poetry was a crucial part of this process, as I began to bring my feelings and my memories together on the page. I wrote about the journey my sister and I had made to Gibraltar to arrange for a gravestone, the year after my parents' death; I wrote about the sadness I felt watching two strangers: a mother and grown-up daughter who were clearly friends; and I wrote a long series of villanelles in which I directly addressed my mother and spoke of my loss. These were among the most powerful poems I had ever written, as I soon found when I included them in my public readings. Women from the audience would come to talk with me about their own mothers' deaths and would often thank me for speaking about something they rarely heard addressed.

The grief freed me, for the first time, to know real joy, but it would be untrue to pretend that I simply grieved and lived happily ever after. I have a relationship to public disasters different from most people I know, and I have lost at least one friend because of it. When that friend became very upset at a mountaineering disaster that killed some children who were friends of her son's, I turned on her with venom. "It's not your tragedy," I said, with enough anger to sever our friendship and no power to explain just how presumptuous I found her tears for those relative strangers.

Another consequence of my mother's experience was my exaggerated fear of travel. This mostly was focused on those I loved, rather than myself, although I am still quite afraid of flying. My panic at my lover's departure on a journey has, in the past, led to my virtual hysteria in the airport, a desire to sneak on the plane with her "so we'll die together," or, at the very least, constant phone calls to the airline to track the progress of the plane. Allowing myself to grieve freed me from a lot of this fear, but I still insist on phone calls to announce safe arrival, and I still make sure my partner carries my name and phone number so I will be informed if "anything happens." I do not expect ever to be entirely free of the knowledge that any departure can turn out to be the last.

Even more destructive was the addiction: twenty years of a behavior powerful enough to keep my mother's death at bay left behind a string of broken relationships. When I reached my lowest ebb it was the people I had hurt that haunted me, not my own pain. Even when I no longer needed the compulsive behavior and the drama to mask the pain, the pattern had been set and I had no way of knowing how else to conduct my life. But I found that the more I gave up romantic distraction and a drama-filled love life, the more layers of grief about my mother, and other long-buried pain too, came to the surface.

Sometimes now, when loving seems hard, I find myself crying in a way that feels like that same grief all over again. I feel motherless, alone in the world, and in my mid-forties I become the abandoned child I wouldn't let myself be at nineteen. I know now that the pain will never entirely go away; my task is to coexist peacefully with the fact of my mother's death and her continuing absence. Certain smells, certain moments when I feel unloved, certain aspects of the Christmas rituals, and hundreds of other ordinary details of life, will reopen the wound. But at least now I can let it bleed for a while and go on. At least now I can be open, not only to those painful moments, but also to the many joys of my life.

FOR MY MOTHER, GENEVA

Marilyn Elain Carmen

My mother was a tall woman with skin the color of sand and a smile that shown like the moon over quiet waters. Her voice, when not ravished by mental illness, was soft as an autumn breeze that shakes red and golden leaves from trees. I was always told, even as a small child, that I was a "momma's baby." My aunt Marge still tells me stories of how I'd cry when someone else tried to pick me up.

As my mother's mind became clouded by the disease of schizophrenia, she became abusive towards me, called me names, beat me all night long, paraded herself naked in front of me, and wouldn't allow me to change my underwear. But I still clung to her, trying to get her to love me the way she did before she got sick.

I held onto memories of happier times, remembering the day she let me stir the fudge she was making, or the day she sat beside me in the hospital, reading me a story before my tonsillectomy. It was these memories I held onto when I got beat all night, like the night Momma and Aunt Marge took turns beating me with a gold buckled leather belt. They said I stole some money. "You did it. I know you did it. You no good for nothing ugly black nigga." I didn't know what Momma was talking about. I just wanted her to smile at me.

My mother was kind to me on the last night of her life. Barry, my brother, who was three years younger than my eleven years, was already asleep on our family bed, which was a mattress on the floor in one of the rooms of our apartment. My mother sat in the bathroom with a *Reader's Digest* in her hands. Scanning the pages, she said to me, "Never buy a Dodge car." For many years, I wondered what she meant by those words. At first I thought she was responding to an automobile advertisement; however, I have now come to believe that seeing a car in *Reader's Digest* triggered thoughts as to what almost happened five years earlier in our family car, which was a maroon Dodge.

[101]

My mother and her sister Margaret had planned to collect my brother and me and Marge's son, Calvin, into our car and drive it off the side of a mountain. The plan was thwarted because they could not find the car keys. Perhaps telling me never to buy a Dodge car was her way of saying that she was sorry.

On that last night of my mother's life, I took her hand as she walked down the hall to our bedroom. She walked slowly. The hall seemed so long that night. I knew she was sick, but she was sick a lot so I didn't worry. She had what I have since come to learn were grand mal epileptic seizures. When she started shaking in her sleep, biting her lips, foaming from the mouth, Aunt Marge would tell my brother and me to leave the room and close the door. "Make sure you don't tell a soul," she would say in that firm voice that always scared me. So as a child, my mother's sicknesses appeared normal.

When we reached the bedroom, my mother inched her body down to the mattress. She wore her red plaid skirt and white blouse. Our household was quite disorderly. There was no such thing as dirty clothes and clean clothes, or night clothes. Clothes were just kept either on the floor or thrown in a closet. So most likely I did not change into pajamas. I doubt I even had any.

I was happy about one thing that night before I went to sleep. Barry and I had our Halloween costumes and were ready to go "trick or treating." Our costumes were in a bag on the living room floor. Momma had gone shopping for them earlier that day. I remember her saying how tired she was after walking downtown to get them. I can see her now, smiling a little as she said, "I wanted you and Barry to have them in time for Halloween."

Before I closed my eyes to sleep that night, I decided I would get up early the next morning and make some Wheatena for my mother. I had never cooked on the stove before, but I wanted to make my mother happy by making her breakfast. I wanted to surprise her.

I awakened first the next morning which was unusual. My mother was always the first to rise. She was a morning person. But that morning she lay still beside me. I coughed, hoping that would stir her. Nothing happened. I wanted her to wake up, but didn't want her to be mad at me for waking her, so I coughed again. I cleared my throat. Nothing happened. Finally, I called to her, "Mommy. Mommy." Still she did not move or answer.

She was lying on her stomach with her face turned toward the mattress. I clutched her body and turned it over. She lay on her back, frozen. A stream of white foam trailed from her mouth. I ran screaming from the apartment.

When Cousin Clara told me that my mother was dead, the first thought that entered my mind was, "Oh no. God. Now Aunt Marge is really going to beat me bad." Aunt Marge told me regularly that I was going to worry my mother to death because I cried so much. Instead of being mad at me, Aunt Marge went into the kitchen and made bacon and eggs for breakfast. She and Barry ate. I could not eat I sat in the living room by myself, crying.

No one talked to me about my mother's death. No one cried with me. Relatives from various parts of the country were in and out of our apartment. With them they brought their furs, some food, and money, which they gave to Aunt Marge to buy me and Barry some "suitable funeral clothes."

Aunt Marge took Barry and me shopping. Instead of taking us home to dress for my mother's funeral, Aunt Marge took us to the movies. By the time we got back to our apartment, the funeral was over. Relatives were gathered, but no one looked sad except my grandmother who said, "Geneva looked just like she was all asleep in pink."

The next day, my father, who had remarried without my mother's knowledge, drove from his home in Roselle, New Jersey to take my brother and me back home with him. He did so to keep us from going into an orphanage.

As I look back over the last thirty-six years of my life, I realize that I have spent much time and energy attempting to avoid the issue of my mother's death, trying to cover it up in my mind. I had never really allowed myself to believe that she was dead, even though I watched as two strange men entered our apartment that morning, covered her face with a sheet, and carried her on a stretcher out of the door.

Still I didn't believe it. I had never grieved. No one talked to me about my mother's death. I could cry with no one.

Everyone acted as though nothing of significance had occurred. Like it was a normal thing for a child to wake up and find her mother dead beside her. No one seemed to be able to help me understand that Momma was gone, so I just kept looking for her.

I imagined I saw her in everyone I met. I wanted everyone to be like my mother was before she got sick. I wanted everyone I knew to be nice to me. I wanted the men in my life to treat me the way I had wanted my mother to treat me, the way she had treated me before she became ill. But all I received from these men were black eyes, skinned knees and a more shattered sense of self-worth.

I began to take mood-altering drugs. And I took them for fifteen years, along with anything I could get to drink: wine, beer, whiskey. Not glasses, I mean bottles. I lived in bars, looking for something to drink, or looking for the man currently in my life, or looking for a new man. Always high. Always looking.

When the pills and booze didn't mask enough, or maybe when they covered up too much, I'd become crazy, staying in bed for days, weeks. I believe I kept thinking, "If I get sick enough, if I get crazy enough, my mother will come back and take care of me." But she never came.

One day I went into a screaming fit and had myself committed to Marlboro State Hospital. I stayed there for a week. The potholder making. The pill lines. The food. I remember talking to a psychiatrist once. He told me, "Mrs. Carmen, you can go home for the weekend if you stop crying so much."

I began my forty-eighth year still searching. My mother died on October 30, and the autumn was always an extremely difficult time for me. Starting in August, my moods began to shift into a more depressive state, and by October I was crying every day, extremely depressed and fearful, afraid to cross the street alone, afraid to walk past a tall brick building for fear it would fall on me. When I walked with my youngest daughter, Crystall, I grabbed her hand as we crossed the streets.

One afternoon that autumn I asked my dear friend Robert if I could talk to him about my mother. As I looked into his eyes, I knew that after all these years, this was the person I could talk to. Not only did I tell Robert the story of how my mother died, but I relived that night. Robert squeezed my hand as tears flooded from my eyes.

Finally, with Robert's help and patience, I figured it out. All these years, I had been looking for my mother, looking for someone to explain to me what happened to my mommy. I had been looking for a way to grieve without destroying myself in the process. I needed to get rid of the guilt, to find a way to live out my life without attempting to pay for the fact that my mother became ill and died before she could live.

Robert suggested we have a celebration in honor of mother's life. At first I didn't understand what he meant by that. What was there to celebrate? I was afraid, but I nodded my head in agreement. By the next day I began to feel less afraid. I decided to borrow a dress. I rarely wore dresses, nor did I own stockings. But this was a celebration for my mother, and I wanted to look special. I purchased lipstick along with my new stockings. It felt strange looking through the cosmetics that I had not worn in fifteen years. I chose red lipstick to match my black and red dress.

When I arrived back home, I began to think about what I wanted to take with me for the "celebration." The first thing I decided on was Momma's high school picture. The picture is signed, *With much love, Geneva.* As I took the picture down from the dresser, I thought of how beautiful she was. Sometimes when Crystall smiles, I am reminded of my mother's lovely smile. For her graduation picture, my mother wore a black sweater topped with a white collar. Her hair was cut short and curled just above her ears. Small bangs touched her forehead. Momma's eyes were almost bright, with only a hint of what would happen to her in the future.

I scanned my bedroom walls for another picture for the celebration. I removed a photograph of some of the children who had attended the nursery school that my mother ran from our home during the mid-1940s. My mother, who was part Native American, African and English, had developed an integrated nursery school center, attended by both Black and White children. It is Christmas time in the photograph. The children are wearing costumes designed and handmade by my mother for a Christmas pageant that she had created.

I wrapped the two pictures in tissue paper and tied them with a pink ribbon. Pink was Momma's favorite color. I placed them in a bag, and I also included Momma's high school and college transcripts.

I took special care in dressing the next morning. Robert told me I looked beautiful as soon as he saw me. I thanked him as I sat down and opened my bag with Momma's special things. First I unwrapped the pictures, placing the tissue paper and ribbon on the chair beside me. I showed Robert the pictures, told him what I knew about her high school and her college scholarships. I told him about her nursery and about how she liked playing the piano for the nursery school kids and for me and Barry. I told him how we used to sing church songs around the piano, how much fun she was, how kind she was, before she got sick.

While I was sorry when the celebration was over, I felt happier and more connected than I had ever felt in my life. The next day was Halloween. Instead of being depressed and fearful, I enjoyed watching Crystall as she dressed up to go out "trick or treating." Then I went to my room and watched something funny on television.

I now carry within me the positive forces sparked by that celebration two years ago. I know that my life and the way in which I attempt to live it is a continuous celebration of my mother's short life, for she lives in me.

SMALL COMFORTS
An Essay on Mary

Alison Townsend

We think back through our mothers if we are women....
    –Virginia Woolf

Begin here. With the facts. She was my mother, Mary. She diedof breast cancer in December 1962, just a few weeks before Christmas. She was forty-three years old and had been ill intermittently for three years. I was nine and a half and, though she had been sick enough to go to the hospital several times, I was unprepared for her death. Even now, almost thirty years later, I still feel unprepared, obsessed, and searching, still struggling to answer the question I first voiced as a nine year old girl: "Why did my Mommy die?"

According to my father, my mother first contracted fibrocystic breast disease about three years before she died of cancer. This would have been in 1959, when I was six years old and my brother Steve and sister Jenny four and three, respectively. We lived in rural eastern Pennsylvania, on five acres of mixed pasture and woodland my parents named "Wild Run Farm." It was the first house they had ever owned and though they were pressed for money, it was a happy place, a green, enchanted world where nature worked her spell upon us, protecting those who were so soon to be exiled from its paradise.

From what my father tells me, my mother was hospitalized twice, each time for excision of fibrotic nodules. The operations were successful, the findings benign. In their "enormous relief over the innocuous nature of her illness," my parents' "shield was down," my father said twenty years later, in a heart-rending letter in which he tried to answer my questions about my mother's final illness and death.

But sometime in 1961 a lump or nodule must have recurred. In the early summer, my mother again entered Allentown Hospital, where all three of us kids had been born. This time the findings were more serious. She had a radical mastectomy, followed by radiation therapy. Because she was pre-menopausal, the doctors also performed an oophorectomy and a hysterectomy, operating on the assumption that since the breast tumor might be estrogen-responsive, removing her female parts would prevent (or at least inhibit) the growth of any remaining cancer cells.

My father believes the doctors were right. "For a full year," he writes, "Mary was not only symptom-free, but in vigorous health and spirits." He tells me "she often spoke of it as 'the best year of my life.'" I, in turn, believe what he says. And yet I wonder what it must have been like for her.

Summer 1961. My mother is in the hospital for more than just a few days. But Jenny, Steve and I have not been told she is sick. Surely we sense that something is wrong. But because our parents want to "protect" us, we kids know nothing of the true nature of her illness. Our first cousin Jean, who was a flower girl in my mother's wedding and is ten years my senior, comes to the farm to take care of us while Mommy is in the hospital. I remember lying outside on an old quilt with Jean, "suntanning" myself in imitation of this glamorous older cousin. At one point she lets me brush her hair the way my mother lets me brush hers. When I stop, Jean brushes my hair for a long time, the way Mommy does, then re-braids it and holds me against her for a moment. "I know," she says softly. "I know."

Later I encounter my father in a shadowy part of the house. His study perhaps. Or maybe it is in the front hallway, dominated by the floor register where I sometimes sit on winter evenings, in the small black rocker that was my mother's when she was a child, drying my freshly-washed hair and reading while she plays the piano in the next room. This summer it seems like my father (who has always had time to play Hide and Seek or Fox and Geese with us on long, light evenings after supper) is away constantly. When he is home he's a blur of motion, wolfing down his food and hurrying to the hospital to visit Mommy, often returning only after we are asleep. We are not taken to see her and, though she has been gone only a few weeks, it feels like a long time, in memory the entire summer.

My father, usually sensitive, seems not to see me. But I have something I have to ask him. I feel my chest will burst if

I don't. And so I reach out, tugging at his hand for attention. "Daddy?" I ask, pulling again to make him stop. "Daddy, when is Mommy coming home?" My father glances at me distractedly but lovingly. "Soon," he replies. "Mommy will be back soon." He stoops to hug me, then hurries off again. I believe what he says, but something about his answer leaves me dissatisfied and afraid and I develop an irrational fear of a witch who lives beneath my high-posted rope bed, which my mother slept in as a girl.

But my father's words prove to be true. Soon my mother does come home from the hospital. The morning after her return, on a cool, green-gold day, I find myself alone with her in the living room. She sits on a straight-backed chair, her long full skirt spilling almost to the floor. I walk over and lean companionably up against her. What I really want is to be held in her lap, though at eight I'm getting too big for this. She puts her arm around me. Delighted, the world suddenly right again, I lean closer into her familiar, talcum-scented warmth, and half sit against her thigh.

But something is wrong. My mother flinches at my touch and pulls away for a moment as if I have hurt her. Frightened, I draw back, wondering what I've done. "It's okay, honey," she says quickly, alert to my confusion. "It's just that they took a skin graft from my leg and it's a little sore." "A skin graft?" I ask, puzzled and afraid. "Yes," she says brightly. "It's sort of like a patch, or a band-aid. They attached it over the place where I had the operation to help the skin grow back there."

Or does she even say that much? In truth, I do not remember the words (though I know she said something), only the scene itself, like something out of a Victorian mourning picture or the big book of Currier and Ives prints my mother loves. The scene, and the fact that, when I tried to sit in my mother's lap I hurt her. My mother, who had always seemed all-powerful and protective, is suddenly vulnerable to pain. But I don't understand what causes the pain, or even where it exists in her body. I certainly don't realize that, even as she wraps her arm around me in a warm hug, the movement hurts her again, pulling at the skin grafted over the raw places where her breast had been.

My mother began radiation therapy, and it was effective for a while. But as my father writes, "In the early summer of 1962 the cancer recurred, first as nodules in the skin near the original incision, then, more ominously, as metastatic deposits in her neck." The situation this time was far more serious. My father says he suspects my mother sensed "that she did not have much time of her own left." She was hospitalized in Philadelphia. We kids went to stay with Mommy Doak, our maternal grandmother, in the big stone house on Coulter Street, in the Germantown neighborhood where my mother had grown up with nine brothers and sisters. Even our dogs went with us, a fact which impressed, if not the gravity, then at least the extent of the situation upon me.

On the surface, everything seemed fine. We loved our grandmother's rambling, three-storied house with its nooks and crannies and playroom where two doll houses and a to-scale clipper ship left from my mother's childhood awaited us. My grandmother enrolled us in the library at Germantown Friends School (which my mother had attended), took us to play on the swings and in the sandboxes outside Penn Charter (where all my uncles had gone), to the museums, and on excursions to Wissahickon Park.

I remember in particular one insufferably humid night when I couldn't sleep. My grandmother sat up beside me for hours, rubbing my back with violet water and murmuring, over and over, "It's all right, darling. Everything is going to be all right." What sorts of thoughts must have gone through her mind as she sat there, reassuring her granddaughter, with her own daughter so soon to die?

But there were gaps in the adults' cover-up. My father, who was staying at Coulter Street too, was hardly ever around, once again rushing from his office to the hospital. Once I came upon him talking with my grandmother, his face gray and drawn. Can it be that she held both his hands in her own small white ones? That tears ran down his face? I do not know. There is so much I do not know about what was going on that, memory failing, I fear I invent. But I do know that they fell silent when I entered the room. That there were conversations between adults which were as secret and swirling as the folds in the red velvet drapes that muffled the light in my grandfather's cigar-scented study.

There is a photograph of my mother, taken that summer. She sits beside us on the cool, mossy front steps at 134. She wears a mismatched outfit, striped skirt and print blouse, and, though she often threw on whatever was handy without a thought for what she looked like, there is something about the way the clothes hang on her body which suggests that just putting them on, just sitting there, smiling, acting as if everything was all right, was an effort. Her face is tired and there is silver I don't remember seeing before streaked through her dark blond hair. What I remember is her tiredness, the same tiredness that she spoke of to me, years later, in an active imagination dialogue, saying, in response to my *"Why did you die, Mommy?" "I just got tired, so tired I just couldn't go on, much as I loved you all."* I seem to remember her having to be convinced to join us for the picture, where she looks ill and exhausted, but at the same time strangely luminous.

We were not allowed to visit my mother at the hospital this time either. I don't even know what happened to her during this hospitalization. The one time we were allowed to see her it was from the hospital grounds, through binoculars trained on her fourth story window. She wore a white gown and waved to us. She smiled and looked like herself. One of my uncles took photographs of Jenny, Steve and me looking up at her through the binoculars. Years later, when my grandmother died and family memorabilia was distributed, the photographs came to me. My sister and brother and I look so small and eager and yes, desperate, in the photos. Even as I studied them obsessively, searching for clues, I could scarcely bear to look at our raw and undisguised yearning. I don't think my mother had ever seemed so far away as she did in that moment when the binoculars focused and I beheld her, small and white as one of my own dolls, with so much distance between us.

When it seemed she would never return again, my mother came back from the hospital, smiling and vital, seemingly recovered. And, after a few days more at Mommy Doak's, we returned to Wild Run Farm. It was midsummer, and the land seemed glorious and green and timeless, the one unchanging element in our disrupted lives. My father made a tape of us one night over dessert, proud of his new recorder with the little silver microphone that dangled like a fish. Somehow every summer at Wild Run Farm seems summed up in that evening of sweet peaches, fireflies flickering over the lawn, and my mother's voice (which I can no longer remember) speaking softly, shyly, into the recorder.

But it was not to remain that way for long. My father had accepted a new job with Geigy Pharmaceuticals; my parents couldn't afford not to move. And so we left Wild Run Farm. To us kids, piled in the back of Grey Car with our dogs and pet rabbit, Babe, it was an adventure. I don't think we even looked back as the car pulled out onto the dirt road for one last time. But my mother? I believe that though she went along with the move, in her typically courageous and uncomplaining fashion, she also left something of herself behind at the farm, the part that perhaps could not be comforted by anything other than that green and fertile place. How else is it I know with such certainty that the ghost a young couple who now own the farm have described to my father is my mother, still searching for peace in the last place she knew it?

From the time of our move on, my mother's story accelerates, speeding up the way the cancer cells had begun to metastasize in her body. Memories and images pile up quickly, one frozen shot merging seamlessly into another like those trick books where flipping the pages makes the picture move. Here is my mother, encouraging me to go out and play kickball when the girls on the block knock on our door and ask me out. Here she is, watching out the window while my father teaches me to ride the black Schwinn she'd given me for my birthday the preceding May (I do not know she is too weak to help me herself); delighting in finding a second-hand couch (our first); walking out the route I will ride to school with me before school starts (just to make sure I've got it down); taking me to meet Miss Marshall at Hilltop School for Girls, where I will resume my piano lessons every Wednesday after school; talking to Miss Coster about violin lessons, renting the beautiful instrument in its velvet-lined case; singing with the dogs; giving me a wicker basket for the front of my bike; braiding my hair; tucking us into bed; singing; playing the piano the way she always has; walking to meet us kids each day on our way back from school (though she is already weakening); posing in a formal studio portrait of the family with a look of such serenity that my father will later marvel repeatedly, "Can you believe that picture was taken just six weeks before she died?" And here she twirls in front before us in a new blue calico shirtwaist dress my father has gotten her at B. Altman's, her laughter ringing out like a girl's. It is the dress she will be buried in.

My mother is dying. At Memorial and Sloan-Kettering hospitals the doctors tell my father there is nothing they can do to save her. He later writes, "It was the first time I had been forced to face it, to hear it in words." He cannot tolerate it. He knew of an experimental immunotherapy program at the Cleveland Clinic. He persuades my mother to go out there. Sometime in November my mother enters the hospital for the last time, promising us she will be home in time for Thanksgiving.

Later she revises this — she will definitely be back for Christmas. Meanwhile, life goes on in the house at Bellewood Avenue. Jenny, Steve and I attend school. Steve collects Golden Guns. Jenny and I play Barbies. I learn to play a screechy version of *Twinkle, Twinkle, Little Star* on the violin in preparation for our January recital. Snow falls for the first time, and we learn about sledding in town, flying down Hill Street atop large pieces of cardboard.

But underneath this as-normal-as-possible surface, cracks and fissures start to appear. Steve begins to wet his bed again. When I say my prayers at night I ask for Mommy "to get better and come home soon," only to be horrified by the intrusive and seemingly autonomous wish that she die. And my sister? My sweet-tempered, blond-haired sister, who at six resembles a chubby angel? What does she think? What do any of us think? There is a veil of silence and secrecy around our mother which we cannot penetrate. We talk of a time "when Mommy gets home" or "comes back," but we never articulate the fears underneath.

My mother reaches out to us in every way she can. She writes us postcards of a sentence or two which we fall upon eagerly, hungry for both the novelty of receiving mail and hearing from her. She sews us things — little felt donkeys with blanket saddles and embroidery floss manes and tails, and for us girls, strawberry lapel pins, each seed stitched in delicate gold — from kits my father must have purchased for her in the hospital gift shop.

My mother also reads over our Christmas wish lists and sends my father out to purchase the one item we each want most. Jenny's is a Thumbelina baby doll, Steve's a big stuffed bear, and mine a Madame Alexander doll from the Little Women collection, not Jo (my heroine) but the blond-haired Amy I'd dreamed over in the Sears Christmas catalogue. Gifts from beyond the grave, they are under the tree for us on Christmas at my grandmother's house. Each one bears a tag that reads: "With all my love, Mommy." But I can never bring myself to play with the doll.

With Christmas and Mommy's promised return approaching, I begin to work on her present. I decide to make her dinner napkins, with her initial, "M" — for "Mommy" not "Mary"— embroidered in each corner. Working with what I have, I make my mother's "napkins" from old white sheets. I tear them down to what seems about the right size, then "embroider" an "M" on each one — with ordinary light blue thread. They must have been terribly awkward. But I thought they were beautiful, my desire to bring her happiness spelled out in each stumbling stitch. I make five, one for each member of our family. Then I wrap them in tin foil because it, too, seems beautiful to me — all silver and sparkle — tie the package up with one of my old hair ribbons, and hide it away carefully.

I still remember how intently I worked on those napkins and how satisfied they made me feel. I had made something — a surprise — for Mommy for Christmas. And the making made her return seem real, tangible in the way nothing else had been that whole fall. It didn't occur to me that she would never see them.

My mother dies in her sleep, a little after midnight on December 16, shortly after my father shows her a photograph of us kids. And, when I walk home alone from school late one gray afternoon and see my father's red Austin 850 — which has been gone for months — parked by the curb in front of our house, I know my mother isn't with him.

"A red car and no sun," was how I put it, trying to capture the feeling of that moment in an essay I wrote at seventeen. And time has not changed the picture or dimmed the memory. I walk, propelled by forces larger than myself, toward a red car and a house of grief. My father takes us all upstairs, saying, "I have something I need to tell you children." But before he can speak I say, "I know, Daddy. I know," the words breaking in my throat like shards of glass that dissolve into tears.

Later our house becomes a whirlpool of activity. Neighbors we barely know rush in and out with casseroles. Aunt Betty comes out from her apartment in the city to take care of us kids and help with all the arrangements. She braids my hair and I am shocked by how closely her hands resemble my mother's. She and my father argue over both what dress my mother will be buried in and what dresses Jenny and I will wear to the funeral. My father wins on both counts, and I am glad. My mother is buried in the dark blue calico; Jenny and I wear the blue corduroy jumpers she made for us, clothes my aunt maintains aren't dark enough for a funeral. I cry. Jenny and Steve cry. My father cries. We all cry as if we will never stop.

Just before the ceremony, my father and Reverend Kendall take us kids into the small chapel at South Presbyterian Church to make our farewells. My mother lies in a pink satin-lined coffin with elaborate gray scrolling on the outside. Her hands are folded across her chest. A halo of pink tea roses from my father curves above her head. She is very still, as if she is sleeping, and she looks so much like her ordinary self that I can't help but watch to see if her chest is moving. Reverend Kendall takes us closer, right up to the edge of the casket. "Do you want to say goodbye to your mother?" he asks. Jenny and Steve pull back in terror, clinging to my father's hands and sobbing.

I want to do the same thing. But Reverend fixes his kindly gaze upon me and asks, "What about you, Abby?" And there is nothing to do but step forward. Reverend explains: "Your mother isn't here anymore. Her spirit is at peace with God, in heaven. These are only her earthly remains."

His words mean nothing to me. She looks like my mother, is my mother. I step up to the coffin which rests upon a raised walnut dais. I pause for a moment and look over the edge. My mother lies below me, still and silent and, according to the Reverend, gone. But she looks so much like herself. I recognize every line in her face, how her brows curve in a firm but gentle line, the way her hair frames her face in soft curls as if she herself has just taken out the bobby pins she used to wind it up in. She is infinitely familiar and infinitely strange. Terrified, I stand, poised on the brink of an abyss from which there is no return, then lean down and quickly kiss her forehead. Her skin is cold. Touching it, a chill seems to enter my body. I shrink back, away from the one who gave life to me, who has carried me as no other ever will, aware for the first time of the enormous difference between the living and the dead. I shrink back, away from some intuitive knowledge that, having kissed the dead, I am doomed to forever look back, carrying the memory of the underworld in my body, like curse, or amulet, or blessing.

I don't know how we get through the funeral. The church fills with people — aunts, uncles, cousins, people I don't know. As my father says later, "Everyone loved Mary." Words are spoken. Hymns must be sung. Surely my grandmother, that marvelous protectress, is there. But I do not remember her, just a confused progression of faces ordinarily glimpsed only at Thanksgiving or on visits to Coulter Street. All I can recall with clarity is standing in the front pew with my father and brother and sister, all of us sobbing aloud. I weep until I can hardly breathe. Someone hands me a blue Kleenex, which I wipe my face with until the flimsy paper falls to pieces in my hand. But the crying does not stop. It will be a long time before the crying stops. It will never stop completely, but instead take up residence within me as emptiness filled with the whimpering of a small wounded animal, forever vulnerable, forever undefended, forever embedded with a sorrow I can't quite name.

Of the burial itself I remember almost nothing. Only the garish unreality of the fake green "grass" which conceals the mound of freshly dug earth. The rectangular pit in the ground. The flowers, so many flowers. The moment when the coffin is lowered into the cold, hard ground of December. Later my father says something about the stone he has chosen, a simple curved bench of rose marble. There are two slender birches leaning gracefully nearby. Somehow I like having them there, like the two dryads standing watch over her grave.

After the funeral I hear my father ask Aunt Betty and Aunt Bea if they want any of her clothes. He stands in front of the open closet. They look stricken and seem to pull back, as if Mommy's illness — and death — were contagious. "I guess I'll have to send them to Goodwill," my father says, his shoulders hunched and voice breaking. As difficult as it is for me to imagine my aunts wearing my mother's clothes, I feel a hot stab of anger. Why couldn't they take something, even if they just gave it away when they got home?

Later I open the dark, varnished door of the closet and stand there for a moment, looking at the rack of clothes, each outfit so familiar it seems to bear the imprint of her body. Here are the simple calico dresses with rickrack around the neck which she sewed herself to save money. Her fancy dress of blue and green and purple material that feels like silk. And the soft gray coat of fake fur lined with pink satin, a present my father once brought back to her from a trip to Canada. When I look at it, I see my mother trying it on in the kitchen at Wild Run Farm. She holds a Black Cat cigarette in one hand and looks tall and glamorous as a movie star.

Reaching out to caress the shimmering fur, I glance around surreptitiously, then enter the closet and shut the door. Inside, surrounded by folds of fabric still bearing her scent, I pull the clothes around me and breathe in deeply, as if the scent, inhaled, will bring her back. I wrap myself in her garments as I can no longer wrap myself in her arms and stand there for a long time, my tears soaking the cloth until, exhausted by grief, I dissolve into sleep. My father finds me there later, my cheek pillowed against her sparkling silver party shoes he takes to Goodwill the next morning.

Time collapses in on itself and we are at my grandmother's house for Christmas. Then we are home again. It must be only a matter of days, because we are still on school vacation. I wake up every night, screaming and sobbing the moment I remember — Mommy is gone. She is dead. She's never coming back. I run to their old room where my father now sleeps alone and curl up in bed beside him. We hold one another and cry until we fall asleep. At some point he must carry me back to my own bed. I wake up there every morning, alone, next to the doll house she made for me on the jigsaw, in that bed that sheltered her dreams as a girl.

School begins again. At first I refuse to go, just as I have refused to return to the church where my brother and sister sing in the choir, and Reverend Swan, a idealistic young assistant pastor with little understanding of children, has given me a Bible. I immediately deface it, scribbling inside the front cover, "I'm never going back to this church that took my mother away." I kick and scream until I'm nearly hysterical. My father finally gives up and lets me stay home from school. But the next day, through some decision of my own, I go. My fourth grade teacher, Mrs. Carter, says, "I want you all to give Abby a very special welcome back, boys and girls." She makes me stand, cringing, at my desk, while they do so. I've never felt so ashamed. For a moment I hate my mother for dying and exposing me to this.

But I have become invisible; no one says anything to me afterwards. Out on the playground, other girls ignore me, suddenly busy with friendships which seem to have sprung up since I was gone. Only Jay Dickey, the bully of my block, says something as we walk home that afternoon on opposite sides of the street. "I'm sorry about your mother," he says awkwardly, when he gets to his house. It is the gentlest moment I've experienced all day. "It's okay, Jay," I call back across to him. "It's okay." It isn't, of course. But I am so moved and embarrassed I don't know what else to say.

Somehow we fall into a routine of going on without my mother. My father works, takes an evening class at The New School, and hires a housekeeper to look after things and prepare regular meals. We attend school. I give my violin recital, painfully aware that only my father is watching me. Sometimes we go into the City on weekends, visiting my aunt, or going to museums with my father. In my ravenous need for affection, it seems I am always asking him to buy me something — a Barbie doll, a copy of *Nobody's Girl* by Hector Malot, a little wooden horse rolling over and kicking up its hooves. Nothing fills the space.

My favorite times are mornings. At this hour my mother

comes to me, visiting in the form of clear, gold light which spills through the sheer white curtain onto my bed as I make it up, straightening the sheets into hospital corners as she taught me. As I smooth out the coverlet she made only the spring before by sewing a duvet of strawberry-printed cotton over an old blanket, it seems that she is with me, just on the other side of the bed, talking to me, helping me. These visitations feel miraculous and fill me with warmth.

Mornings are also a time of trial. My father struggles to braid my hair. It was always my mother's job and, while others have been doing it in her absence, I still haven't learned to braid it myself. My father tries, but he's all thumbs and it obviously isn't going to work. Finally he says, "I'm sorry, Honeybun. I think we're going to have to go have it cut." I'm desolate at the thought of losing my braids. Long hair has been my identity for most of my life. But he's right. There's nothing else to be done. He takes me downtown to a beauty shop where a woman with long, lacquered nails whacks each braid off with one, irrevocable slash of her shears. Seeing my stricken look, she says, "You want to keep them, honey?" I nod, mute, and am handed a blue net bag swimming with silky ropes. I keep them in my bureau for a long time, looking at them occasionally like a part of myself that is gone forever. It will be many years before I wear my hair long again.

On the weekends we visit my mother's grave at Kensico Cemetery, standing around the still-raw earth in a circle and reciting the Twenty-third Psalm: "The Lord is my shepherd, I shall not want . . . ." The ancient and beautiful words form a soothing ritual. Just speaking them seems to bring my mother, in all her own "goodness and mercy," very close to us. Once there is a rectangular arrangement of holly and ivy laid over her grave. A gift from Bea, it resembles a blanket, something to keep my mother warm as she sleeps.

Sometimes, overcome by grief, I ask my father to explain why Mommy died. None of his answers are very satisfactory and I have to find my own solutions. One day at school I wander alone along the chain link fence that circles the grounds, my arms wrapped around me, my shorn hair blowing in the stiff breeze off the Hudson. I walk without seeing, eyes on the ground, which is scattered with faded candy wrappers. Suddenly a small, perfectly oval, black stone catches my attention. I lean down and pick it up. It is smooth and comforting and grows warm in my hand. I turn it over and over, imagining that I could have it made into a locket. I keep the stone for a long time, carrying it with me everywhere, its smooth blackness crystallizing my grief.

Life goes on, involuntary, inevitable as breathing. Spring comes, and my father has been introduced to the woman he will marry that summer. We visit my mother's grave less and less frequently, then finally not at all. In July we are sent away to Cape Ann, where Betty and Bea have rented a beach house. Years later, Betty writes me that it was something my mother and Bea had planned together. Her words stick in my throat, jagged and beautiful as the shells we collected at Annisquam. So she believed she might live. Had hoped to be there with us as we scrambled over rocks and through tide pools, healing together in the sun and sea and salt.

When my sister and brother and I come "home" from Cape Ann at the end of the summer it is to a new house, two new stepbrothers we like but barely know, and a new "mother." Most of the furniture we remember has vanished, along with other treasures such as "The Christmas Garden," a collection of antique animals for beneath the tree from my grandmother's house. The atmosphere is confused and tense, a situation which will continue until my father and stepmother finally divorce, fifteen years later.

In the new house my nightmares return, dominated by vampires, which surely represent the underworld that is still so close. I become afraid of the dark, and get hysterical whenever my father and Shirley go out in the evening, clinging to them, begging them not to go, for the last time my father and mother had walked out a door into darkness one of them never came back. They send me to a psychiatrist, who terrifies me even more.

Afraid that the candy the doctor offers me contains "truth serum," I say almost nothing during my sessions with him. Instead, I build a plastic model of a horse I name Chestnut Hill. If the doctor bothered to ask about the origins of the name, he would learn it was the big, gentle gelding my mother had arranged for me to take long-dreamed-of riding lessons on two springs before. But he doesn't ask. And I don't volunteer any information. Instead, he prescribes Librium, a powerful tranquilizer, which my father gives me when "the parents" go out, telling me the pastel pills that look like Easter candy will make me feel "less afraid."

Forced to create my own rituals for grief, I begin a secret, fictional diary about a little girl and her mother. Setting it in 1933, I "illustrate" the diary with pictures from my stepmother's magazines that look old-fashioned to me. One that makes a particularly strong impression on me features a mother and daughter in a sunny kitchen dominated by an old wood range. I glue the picture into my diary and write underneath it, "After school today, Mommy and I made cookies together." Each week I fold my entries carefully in an empty cottage cheese container and bury it in the garden. I call the containers "time capsules" and believe that someone will find them someday and learn the truth. It doesn't occur to me until years later that in the act of creating the "diary," I was burying the dead in the only way I knew how to. Those scraps of folded paper and magazine pictures I passed off as my own were like seeds that I planted, opening later into the story that is my life as it has bloomed even without her.

That I "survived" my mother's death is obvious, for who sits here typing these words onto a softly glowing computer screen but me? I have done more than survive. Two-thirds of my life have now passed without her as a reference point, and nearly all my major accomplishments and losses have occurred without her knowledge. My missing her is now marked by cycles and specific events. I find myself thinking of her every autumn after Halloween, when the death of the year echoes her own final illness and death. I think of her during times of extreme need as when, hospitalized for depression, I sob to a friend, "If only my mother were here. She would know what to do." And I think of her at moments when I suddenly wish there was something she could know about from my present life, even if it is so simple a thing as my shy, spotted cat, a sweet creature I am certain she, with her own love for cats, would appreciate. My mother will never meet my husband or read my poetry. She will never be a grandmother to my children. She will never know that I keep a box of her pastels in my desk, or that I have grown into at least something of the artist she helped me dream I would become.

But perhaps she knows all these things. For on another level, she (or rather the fact of her absence) is with me constantly. I am forever different from my women friends who still have their mothers. I am not the same woman I would have been if she'd lived. And I did not, after the age of nine, have the same girlhood. But as to whether either would have been better or worse, I cannot say. All I can say with certainty is that I am haunted by her. That there is a rent, a tear, a rip in the fabric of my life that can't ever be completely sewn up or patched over, but which lets in both the darkness that is the underworld and a world of astonishing — the only word which can describe it is celestial — light. That my mother is both with me and not with me, alive and gone. And, that though these words begin to tell some small part of the story, it is a story I will probably be telling all my life — of a girl and her mother and the love which connects them, like a strong rope, or an umbilical cord, running faithfully between this world and whatever world comes next.

VISITATIONS

IS IT THE TIME OF THE CLOCK WITHOUT HANDS?
(an Ode to the death of my mother)

Daisy Aldan

What time is it?
Is it the time of the clock without hands?

Under the arches on the rocks sit the silent fishermen
        who catch no fish. A sailboat without sails, white
rood darkening the sky, glides like a vessel
        bearing the dead across the threshold.
On the shore lurks the demon, open-mouthed and scaled.
Ducks waddle alert to the fangs of the dog.
I too am alert to the potential dog, prepared at
the first sign of danger to waddle into the sanctuary of
        my element, the water.
(Woe to those who sleep out of their element!)
Glorious the dark water where we may perform our
        rituals, the ducks and I.
I swim among flames of light toward the ladder.

In the Temple of Jerusalem in a sea of flames,
        I lit a candle in a mistaken ritual.
– For whom do you light this candle? – asked the Rabbi.
– For my mother. –
– She is dead? –
– No! –
– These, are candles, for the dead! –
Well, it was a matter, only of a little time.

When will I cease lighting candles for you, my mother?

On this death anniversary, I light the Friday candles
        as you taught me in your kitchen:
One for my dead grandfather, Shmul Leib, composer of

songs for the synagogue,
one for my grandmother, my namesake, Alta Hadassah, who
        radiated light in darkness;
for Papa, Aunt Fayga, and Uncles Schloime, Mendel and Harry,
and for each of the twenty-three aunts, uncles and cousins
        murdered in the gas chambers;
entreating them to greet you there, Esther Hamalkah,
        which means, *The Queen.*

Wherever death is commemorated, I commemorate;
        Wherever prayers are prayed, I pray:

In Bombay I performed Poojahs, and in your name cast
        flowers into the Arabian Ocean:
In rock-hewn caves, I kneeled before a thousand Buddhas,
even Lingams, and implored the three-headed Shiva,
Krishna, Kali, Goddess of Death, to shield you from harm.
In the Pyramid at Gheza, rising from all fours in the
        King's Chamber, I saw
within the open marble coffin, your face of silence,
a bit of white lace falling over your lovely brow.
I joined the phantom mistletoe procession under
the arkite pillars at Avesbury, and heard
your voice resonating from the granite boulders,
and sought you in the shadows where the dead
        return to tell us of themselves.

I have lit candles in the hill monasteries of Mistra,
in 365 small adobe Orthodox churches on remote islands,
before ikons and oil lamps near Cyclopian caves,
and scattered myrtle leaves around Apollo Kore
in the black marble temple at Bassai, facing east:
At Delphi, I made a sacrificial fire of a swan's
feather, dead bird, rose petals, to conjure the Pythia
and beseech her to guide you untormented to the gods.
In electrified crypts of Romanesque churches where
        spirits of martyrs convene,
I saw the simple oak coffin just your size, lowered
        on the squeaking hinges.
At crossroad shrines, hillside caves, celtic crosses,

in museums before steles of ancient departed, and
mummies in ornate sarcophagi and in glass cases,
and portraits of Madonnas haloed in gold leaf, I
assumed the pious gesture of veneration, intoning:
– Watch over Esther on her journey to the stars! –

Head veiled or bared, eyes aloft or lowered,
shod or barefoot, standing tall, or prostrating myself
on woven carpets as in the Moslem mosque in Srinigar
before the Shrine of Mohammed's Hair, my forehead
glued to the ground, where I chanted your name;
or sitting in the women's section among the mourners
in the old synagogue in the Venice ghetto
        where I beat my breast in lamentation.
In myriad Gothic cathedrals, I danced a dance of life,
death and rebirth around the Circle Table: I walked
in the procession, ate the Body, drank the Blood,
begged the gentle Jesus to gather you to His breast.
For you I genuflected, kissing the topaz ring on the
index finger of the Archbishop in red satin and ermine
at Aqui Bagni at the Ceremony of the Bells:
On bleeding knees I crawled to the shrine at Fatima
where the Virgin spoke to the children of the world's
        fate and its salvation,
and I entreated Her to warm you in the ample folds
of her blue cloak during those intervals of bitter cold.
I took to fasting on Yum Kippur, and eating
        unleavened bread at the Feast of Passover
where I felt the absence of your mezzosoprano
        welcoming the prophet, Eliohu Hanovi.

– Mameniu, – said my mother as she lay dying,
– Now I will tell you a secret:
        – I speak with angels. –

AN ACCOUNT

Judith McCombs

She's behind me in line, it's a cafeteria somewhere on Sunday, anywhere mothers are taken for outings. I can hear her already, pushing complaints into my ears: Don't these helpings look small, try the nice three-beans, at least try: if she gets near enough she'll be loading my plate with her big peeling hands.

We're alone in the line: only her voice carries, picking and prodding, I know it by heart. Between our white trays the stainless steel bars are shining. Around us swabbed floors and wide railings; behind the steamed food, a thin counterboy waits in pressed whites, hearing, not hearing, gnawing the side of his thumb. Ahead, the skinny white lilies are banked by the register, waiting for us.

Now she's caught up beside me, in color: dressed from a snapshot some Easter before, the orange-and-blue jersey she stitched, its bright bands widening over her stomach and breasts, like two women there. Her stringy specked hair is pinned back for the picture; her head looks smaller, but she's always been taller than me. Her eyelids are clawed and crusted, hurt scales like a turtle's loose folds; her eyes have that sullen hurt stare I remember. Her hands are touching and clutching my purse, she insists I didn't take nearly enough. I look at her portions, she's right, they aren't enough, and then at the register lilies, leftover from service.

As she offers to count up my change I turn back to the pickles, red and orange and bright yellow, thick jars by the silver, and (though I shouldn't get even, not even in dreams) begin to complain, mocking her tones: Won't you take calories and Can't you at least and Nothing's enough: I'm paying for this, I want it rung up, it's all on my account, all.

Alarm; morning. The dreaming slides back, to that place in my head where the pictures line up, like a debt which can never be settled, never enough.

PEBBLES AND STONES

Roslyn Lund

If we can't find her, maybe she never existed.

"Pete, they close the place at five. We'll be locked in. Let's find the office."

"No. This is plot fifty-six. Where else could she be?"

It's spring but there's a drizzle and I'm cold. Our car is parked on the narrow path. We've walked back and forth ten, twenty times. She always does this to me.

Approaching La Guardia I looked down from the plane and saw that other cemetery, the big one studded with stones — the Citibank Building, the World Trade Center, the Empire State, and the tremor started in my stomach. She bought a plot of four graves and demanded that I keep them properly. I didn't come back in three years. She wanted space until her family would surround her. I'll be buried in Seattle where I belong.

She left money to a male cousin, asking that he say a prayer for her every morning and evening for a year. He refused and tried to return the money. I said the prayers myself for a while but they don't count — because I'm female and irreligious. For god's sake. I can't spend my life worrying about a grave.

"It's so long ago. Perhaps she's disappeared. Stones sink."

"That's ridiculous," Pete says. "This one here is marked 1920. She died in seventy, didn't she?"

I wish he would shave off that beard. He's too tall and thin. The gray beard makes him look like an El Greco saint. He's no saint. Neither am I.

She made me promise to pay my respects every year before the High Holy days. I don't keep track of holy days. I couldn't travel across the country every year, I never had the time or money. She was obsessive about neatness, so I paid for "perpetual" care, and they let the plot go to weeds. The big

[129]

stone at her head tilted.

"This country is all corruption," she would say. "Go fight City Hall."

I did. I made a terrible row, wrote to the authorities, made them return the money. They straightened the stone and planted grass, but I haven't been back in seven years.

Pete looks bushed but he won't give up. If he gave up easily he'd have left me like the others. We walk through Weisbergs and Rubinsons and Steins and Sterns. We walk through small iron gates with arches overhead. The Lutsk Congregation. The Sons of Abraham. But we can't find the Arnolds Young Men Association, the fraternal order that gave parties in New York hotels. I went with her once in a white voile party dress that came just above my bony knees. My cousin Eva kissed me and said I was pretty. My mother whispered, "It's only talk. Don't let it go to your head."

But it did go to my head, though I knew I'd never be tall and gorgeous like Eva. I knew even then that I'd be small and sturdy like my mother.

A crow perches on a nearby stone and watches me while I remember beautiful Eva, married to a Kaminsky. She wore filmy sleeves to cover the numbers burned into her arm. My mother didn't want her to kiss me. "Eva was made to do bad things. That's how she survived the camp."

"If we could find the Kaminsky plot. She's right near them."

"I know, I know, you've told me a dozen times."

"I have to tell you, don't I? If you'd been here before I wouldn't have to, would I?"

The crow caws as I speak. Pete is trying not to smile. "Sonya, just try to calm down. You're getting all hyped up."

My mother was luckier than Eva. She got out of Europe just in time, and on the way she visited aunts in Paris and London.

"Just imagine. I saw the Eiffel Tower and Stonehenge when I was only fourteen. My sister Ruth was smart. She sent for me because she knew what was coming."

Ruth Kaminsky, the housekeeper who married the boss. Her stepchildren taught my mother dirty words for simple objects. They laughed at her and she wanted only to be like them. When she could afford it she bought graves as close to them as she could get.

"If we could find the office they'd tell us."

"We'd get lost looking for the office." Pete is worried. He always thinks I'll fly apart.

"If we were lost in hell you wouldn't ask directions at a gas station."

He shrugs and walks ahead with his usual swagger. Where is the Kaminsky family, the ones who sang? They all played the baby grand piano, even Harry, the oldest, who never took a lesson. My mother heard him as she cleaned and cooked for her keep. "Three notes and a syncopated bass, repeated until he drove me crazy."

I wish the crow would shut up.

I met Harry over coffee at Rumpelmayer's on my infrequent trips to New York. We discussed the care of the graves, his responsibility and mine.

"Did I ever tell you about my cousin Harry?"

Pete doesn't answer. He's tall enough to see over the stones. I'm lost in them. I run after him. The crow follows.

"Harry had a heart attack when he was young, when his wife left him. He was eighty when I last saw him. He told me he had been absolutely faithful to two women for forty years."

"I still take them out to dinner once a week," Harry said.

"Both of them?"

"Separately, of course." He looked down into his coffee. "I can't stop now."

That was seven years ago. I wonder if Harry is still alive. And Eva, who kissed me. Pete shouts triumphantly, "Here they are! The whole family."

I look. "No, no, this is Kutinsky, not Kaminsky."

Pete spins around. "Why did you drag me here? We could have waited. We don't even have a place to sleep tonight."

"I offered to come alone. I don't need you every minute."

"Okay, if you want me to leave, I'll leave."

"Go. If you want to go, then go."

A plane flies over us, scaring the crow away. Now we're the only ones alive in this place. We rented a car and came straight from La Guardia, just ten minutes away. Pete sighs.

"Let's try going this way. Keep close, this is a maze."

I hurry to keep up.

The Kaminskys all played piano so she made me take lessons. I defied her, refused to practice.

"Pete?"

"I'm here, to your right."

I see him. "You're going too fast." I trip on a pebble and fall. My knee hurts.

Clumsy, you never look where you're going. You're asleep standing up. You're a clutz, she would say.

Then would come the curses that sound at home in Yiddish, the language of accumulated fury.

I was exasperating, so was she. Why have I traveled three thousand miles when she found it necessary to beat me —for my own good, she said, her round face as red as her hair. I know I provoked her, I disobeyed, lied, but I didn't send her away from her parents when she was still a child. I didn't choose the man who would leave her, that man she saw in my face.

Maybe I've come to brag because things are going well between Pete and me. I used to think — if your father leaves, what man will ever stay — and yet, finally, I chose a man who would stay.

And there are the children. They both won scholarships, Mother. They're in college now. See how well I'm doing. Despite you.

It's bad luck to praise your children, she says.

"Wait, Pete. I can't get up. My knee — "

You know there's nothing wrong with your knee, she says, so I stand up. I can't see beyond the stones.

"Pete." There's not even an echo. "Where are you?"

I smell weeds. Not a tree here. Spring has exploded back in Seattle but I see no flowers here. A humid wind carries the stench of the city. They lie as close together as they lived —the ex-urbanites. I find the path but our car is gone. No, this is plot fifty, the wrong path. I go back into the stones and call him but my voice is thin. Calm down, try repeating your mantra.

Remember when Pete and I learned to meditate? And our friend Jerry didn't have the money to buy himself a mantra? So we gave him the Maharishi's instructions and told him to make up his own mantra — and he burst into our loft crying, I did it!

For twenty minutes day and night I say it — mantra mantra mantra.

Oh, that's funny. I suppose I'm laughing. This is plot sixty-three. I'm going the wrong way. There's nobody here. I'm lost. I'm alone.

"Pete. Pete. Mother!" Where are you where were you I never could find you.

She's shaking me, her hands on my shoulders. "You slept with him, didn't you! He's not our kind and you went to bed with him."

I pull away.

"He's not the first. I can tell. You're a bum like your father." She slaps me.

I look right back at her. "I'm going away with him."

"Go. You think you'll get rid of me, as though I never existed. You want to wipe me out. You never had a mother. You grew up on the street."

I run through an empty square. Walk, don't run to the exit. You did get away, escaped from that single parent before the epidemic of single parents.

"Remember," she said, "we are separated, not divorced."

Yes, he separated himself from us when I was seven, though he never really lived with us. I remember him saying, "Sonya, do you want me to leave?" I said no but he went anyway. He went and she stayed. Don't tell anyone our business," she said the night he left, wringing her square, reddish hands. I reached out to hold them still. Her hair flamed and she rocked back and forth — and I knew I was a freak because my father left and my mother was caged in a cashier's booth in Harry Kaminsky's movie theatre by day, caged by night in the small apartment.

He left in the fall, and through the long winter I was caged with her. "You're my girl, mine," she said and in her loneliness hugged me too hard and pulled back my hair from my forehead. Her hands smelled of lemon and soap. She didn't want Eva or anyone else to touch me, certainly not a non-Jew.

I call Pete but my throat is sore so I sit on a rusty bench among the Goldsteins who died in 1930, '43, '45. There are more than a dozen of them, practical people, each identically covered with a blanket of myrtle. They must have arranged this long ago around the dining-room table . . . Okay everyone, the consensus is myrtle and let's have an iron bench for visitors.

I see pebbles on one grave. That means recent visitors.

She was practical, too. In the spring she opened the windows to the fire escape and piled all our bedding on the sills. The fresh air came in and she spread her arms wide and breathed deep. How she loved the spring! Nobody ever loved the spring like she did. She freed herself from the apartment, returned to her synagogue, and went to night school.

Like a miracle I was free, too. I went outdoors, found friends, the joy of friends. I did as I pleased, cheated about the time out on the streets, but I was practical, too. I knew enough to be home when she returned.

She learned the language well in night school, hardly a trace of accent, but she misspelled words, so I had to win all the spelling bees. She liked to read so we shared books, spread on the kitchen table, clothes drying from a ceiling rack. On the nights of the Sabbath, newspapers covered her overscrubbed floor. The sink faucets shone like sterling, and she sat leaning on her elbows reading — her freckled chest breathing, plump arms, starched housedress breathing. I can still smell her, feel the energy. I breathed with her. She liked Mark Twain. "He's no Isaac Singer, but he's funny."

I brought her to my library and she brought me to Tolstoy and Dostoyevsky. "My parents read these in Russian before you were born. The Russians weren't funny but they sure could make up plots. Do you think you could ever write?" She laughed but then she touched me on the back. "You don't have to write. Just learn to be a person."

"I am a person."

"I mean a real person."

"If you're real, then I'm real."

That surprised her. "Do you know," she said, quite tenderly, "you've got a big mouth."

Where is Pete? I'm exhausted. Maybe we're locked in.

"Get out. Go. I don't want to see your face ever again. Take that man and go." She pointed and her arm quivered. "To the other end of the world. Go."

We went, to the other end of the land, to the very brink. But one morning I called from a Seattle hospital. "It's me. I thought you'd want to know. You have a granddaughter."

A long silence. "I suppose you're all right."

"Yes."

"Where are you? How do you live? Do you work?"

"We teach, both of us. Pete is a professor."

"Pete? Is he the one you went away with?"

"No, I met Pete here in Seattle. Would you like to visit us?"
No answer.

"May we come to see you with our baby?"

She took her own sweet time before she answered. "Why couldn't you have married a nice Jewish man?"

"You might consider Pete a nice Jewish man."

"Tell me, what's his actual religion?" she spoke loud enough for Pete to hear across the continent.

He said, "Tell her I'm a Druid."

"He says he's a Druid."

"Well," I heard a grudging smile in her voice, telling me: I get the joke but it's no joke. "I guess that's better than a Nazi."

"May we come?"

"I'll let you know."

And she allowed herself to see our daughter, and later our son. We almost became friends. I don't know why that makes me tremble.

We both stopped at the almost. Perhaps she had learned that I hate to be held too close, that my hair, my scalp creeps. Or maybe some time during my childhood I inhaled her stubbornness.

A far-off siren cuts through distant traffic. I can't sit here forever. Is Pete all right? I should look for him but I can't move. I'm cold . . . .

The two sisters are dancing to a Viennese waltz, perspiring, their hair not yet turned gray. My mother says, breathless, "This is called the One-Step."

Ruth laughs, "This is how we danced in Baranow."

"On the Wistula river."

The sisters are hopping. It's a crazy dance. I tell them to cut it out. "That damned anti-Semitic town. A thousand horses couldn't drag you back."

"Sonya's got a big mouth," they say. "Sonya Sonya Sonya," they croon, dancing toward me. They're insane, both of them. If they try to touch me, I'll kill them. If they dare to lay a hand on me, they'll die three times over.

Their voices turn hoarse, and I know that Pete is calling. I'm cold, shivering.

"Pete, I'm here." I stand.

"I can't see you. Speak louder."

I climb up on the bench. He's down among the stones, his hair and clothes disheveled. He comes and clutches my legs.

"Pete, oh Pete." I want to say —"don't ever leave me" — but that always makes him furious, so I speak as decisively as she would speak. "Come, we'll find the office."

I take his hand. He leads me to the car. "This place is demonic."

"But the last place was alive. I saw pebbles on a grave, Pete. That means the plot is alive."

We're riding past stones, a path opens to a road. We find the main building. We come in the back way. The office door is locked and a sign reads, *Closed for the Holiday.*

What holiday?

Pete goes to a large framed map and traces a path with his finger. "Look, there are two sections fifty-six, the left and the right. We should have gone this way."

I see a square marked *Waiting-Room* and remember a small white building, probably a washroom. He finds a scrap of paper and makes a sketch.

We drive up a new path and I remember suddenly — Shavuos! — The holiday of Shavuos — the giving of the law on Sinai. In the spring!

Where did this knowledge come from — this spring festival in my head, in my bones?

The waiting room building needs paint. There's the arched gate — the Arnolds Young Men Association. We stop.

I go through clipped grass to the Kaminsky plot, to the graves of Ruth and her husband Maurice, the head of the clan. *Husband, Father, Grandfather.* Carved in stone.

I spread my arms — the cousins are all here. Harry. Ah, Harry. Died in '82. Beneath his name I read, *A Unique Individual.* Did one of his women suggest that? Did they meet here for the first time, standing over him?

I run, almost dance from one stone to another. Here is Eva

the beauty, the last to die. *Mother. Grandmother. Great-grand-mother.* There are three pebbles on her footstone. Pete frowns, watching me. I know — it's not seemly to be dancing on the Kaminsky graves. I can't help it. I stagger.

Pete points with his chin. "Sonya, look behind you."

I stop moving, turn. I can't breathe. Her headstone is straight, the plot clean. She is covered with ivy. In a corner a vine has wrapped itself around the leaves and a white blossom erupts.

I take a step forward. Whom, what can I embrace? I sit and touch the stone at her feet, bury my hands in the shining leaves. Someone-who-is taking care of this place? I'm leaning — falling forward until my head almost touches the stone. I want, I need to embrace, but there is only air.

Pete pulls me up and puts his arms around me. We hold together.

I'm growing warm. I've stopped shivering.

I pick up two pebbles and place them at her feet.

MOTHER

Grace Paley

One day I was listening to the AM radio. I heard a song: *Oh, I Long to See My Mother in the Doorway.* By God! I said, I understand that song. I have often longed to see my mother in the doorway. As a matter of fact, she did stand frequently in various doorways looking at me. She stood one day just so, at the front door, the darkness of the hallway behind her. It was New Year's Day. She said sadly, If you come home at 4:00 a.m. when you're seventeen, what time will you come home when you're twenty? She asked this question without humor or meanness. She had begun her worried preparations for death. She would not be present, she thought, when I was twenty. So she wondered.

Another time she stood in the doorway of my room. I had just issued a political manifesto attacking the family's position on the Soviet Union. She said, Go to sleep for godsakes, you damn fool, you and your Communist ideas. We saw them already, Papa and me, in 1905. We guessed it all.

At the door of the kitchen she said, You never finish your lunch. You run around senselessly. What will become of you?

Then she died.

Naturally for the rest of my life I longed to see her, not only in doorways, in a great number of places — in the dining room with my aunts, at the window looking up and down the block, in the country garden among zinnias and marigolds, in the living room with my father.

They sat in comfortable leather chairs. They were listening to Mozart. They looked at one another amazed. It seemed to them that they'd just come over on the boat. They'd just learned the first English words. It seemed to them that he had just proudly handed in a 100 percent correct exam to the American anatomy professor. It seemed as though she'd just quit the shop for the kitchen.

I wish I could see her in the doorway of the living room.

She stood there a minute. Then she sat beside him. They owned an expensive record player. They were listening to Bach. She said to him, Talk to me a little. We don't talk so much anymore.

I'm tired, he said. Can't you see? I saw maybe thirty people today. All sick, all talk talk talk talk. Listen to the music, he said. I believe you once had perfect pitch. I'm tired, he said.

Then she died.

MY MOTHER'S BRAIN

Patricia Flinn

For the past couple of months now I've been thinking a lot about my mother's brain. It's sort of an obsession, I guess, because no matter how hard I try, I can't seem to get the damn thing out of my head. Even at work down at the General Store I think about it, when I'm slicing people's cold cuts and wrapping up their ham sandwiches. Twice I got so confused I almost cut three of my fingers off in the slicing machine. And once when the place was packed to the rafters with customers, and I was doling out bowls of clam chowder, I got so upset seeing it hovering in front of my eyes that I knocked the pot off the stove and almost scalded myself.

At night I even dream of it sometimes. It's always floating up and down in some cloudy, greenish water inside a big thick jar that looks a lot like the jar Steve, my boss, keeps the pickled pigs feet in. Sometimes it looks so real, I can almost smell it. Sort of a combination of formaldehyde and decaying skunk. Once or twice I even woke up with my eyes burning.

Joe, my boyfriend, thinks I should see a shrink. He says I must have a lot of guilt locked up inside me. Guilt that's eating away at my subconscious because I let those doctors do that damn autopsy on her. But personally I think Joe is full of shit. He means well and all, but if you ask me he doesn't really know what he's talking about. It's just all that psychology stuff he's studying in school. His head is filled with it, and sometimes he sounds like a real jerk, especially when he starts quoting Freud, or one of his stupid teachers, or something from one of his dumb textbooks, which he's always underlining in ugly yellow ink.

In all honesty, I really don't pay any attention to him. I just let everything he says go in one ear and out the other. Life's a whole lot easier that way, I think.

But still, I have to admit, sometimes it does make me nervous. I mean, dreaming about my mother's brain so much and all. It's not natural. After all, she's been dead for almost a year now and life's pretty much back to normal again. In fact, except for her brain, I really don't think about her at all. And, to be quite frank —which I know must sound rotten — we were never very close to begin with. I thought she was a pain-in-the-ass. Always complaining and feeling sorry for herself and moping around. It used to drive me crazy. Especially when I'd come home from school all happy and find her sitting in the dark against the wall like some goddamn owl.

"Gee, Ma," I'd say, looking up at her with my big sad eyes. "Why can't you be like those moms I see on television? You know, moms like Donna Reed and Jane Wyman and Harriet Nelson. They're always so happy. Always smiling and baking cookies and going off to P.T.A. meetings and stuff. Why can't you be like them, Ma? Huh, why can't ya?"

Sometimes she'd get so mad she'd come at me with the carving knife.

"You little bitch," she'd scream at the top of her lungs. "You goddamn little bitch. I don't know why I ever had ya."

But all that stuff has absolutely nothing to do with what I'm talking about or why I let those doctors do that autopsy on her. That's a whole different matter entirely.

Back then, I just wanted some facts. Some information. Some basic insights into why my mother died, and what went on inside her head all those years, and whether or not it was anything I might catch one day. You know, like Parkinson's disease or varicose veins or something.

And besides, how was I to know what would happen? I always thought autopsies were performed the same day the person died. How was I to know those doctors were going to stick my mother's brain into some jar and then put it into storage for over a month? I thought they were kidding when they told me that.

"I'm afraid there's going to be some delay," the doctor said. "Your mother's the only brain we have here in the lab right now."

Which was really a surprise to me since no one had ever referred to my mother as a brain before.

"We have to keep her on ice until we get a couple more."

"A couple more what?" I asked.

"Brains," he said. "We need at least three."

"Three?" I said, trying to understand. "Why? So they can keep one another company?"

"No," he laughed, thinking I was joking, "To make it worth the pathologist's time to come to do the work. He won't do it just for one brain. There have to be at least three."

"But what if there aren't three?" I asked, getting a bit queasy over the idea that long after my mother's body would be buried under six feet of dirt, her brain would still be floating around in some hospital lab only a mile away from my apartment waiting for some half-ass doctor to show up. "What happens if nobody dies?"

"Oh, I wouldn't worry about that," he said. "This is a hospital. Somebody's always dying here."

And so, what was I to do? At that point the damage had already been done: the autopsy was over, my mother's brain was already in the lab, and her body was already in the funeral home, waiting to be viewed that very night. I couldn't very well ask for her brain back, could I? I mean, what the hell would I do with it? Stick it in her coffin under the satin pillow when nobody was looking?

I tell you, I was really confused. The whole situation was so ridiculous. For the first time I was actually sorry I ordered the damn autopsy.

"Look," I told the doctor. "It ain't right. After all, my mother's dead. She deserves a little respect now. Can't we just force that pathologist to come to the lab. I mean, that's his job, for Christ's sake. That's what he's getting paid for."

"Look, Miss, I'm telling you. He won't come unless there's three brains here. He's a very busy man. He travels all over the state."

"But she's my mother," I insisted. "I can't let you just stick her brain up on some shelf all by itself like that."

"Look, relax," he told me. "Nothing's going to happen to your mother's brain. We're going to take good care of it, and as soon as the other two brains come in, we'll get right to work."

Since I didn't say anything, he probably thought I was upset, because right after that he told me I was perfectly welcome to stop by and chat with him anytime I liked.

"It's against laboratory regulations naturally, but if you want, I'll even take you where we keep your mother's brain. You might enjoy seeing it. I mean, knowing that it's okay and all."

"I think I'll pass," I told him. "I'd much rather remember Mom the way she was."

"Suit yourself," he said.

"What'll happen to it after the autopsy?" I asked. "Will you bury it or what?"

"We'll incinerate it," he said. "That is, unless you're willing to donate it for further use."

"What kind of use?" I asked.

"Oh, research and all," he replied. "You know, the usual stuff. After all, this is a teaching hospital. We're always in the market for good brains."

I said I would have to think about it and then get back to him. But as it turned out, I never did get in touch with him. In fact, I never even read the pathologist's report when it finally came from the lab two months later. I mean, after so much horseshit, how was I to know that they didn't mix things up down at that lab and send me the report of one of those other two brains? Christ, can you imagine if I had read the lousy thing and it said something like, *We're very sorry but after extensive analysis and evaluation, we have come to the conclusion that your mother's brain was 100% healthy and perfectly normal.*

Jesus, that alone would have made my hair stand up. After all, it's one thing knowing that your mother's demented because of medical reasons, and another thing realizing she's simply crazy for no reason.

But besides all that, I had had it at that point. I just wanted to forget all about those doctors and that goddamn autopsy. It was just too nerve-racking. Too depressing. Sitting around thinking about that jar. About my mother's brain. All alone like that on that shelf. In that laboratory. Waiting for that doctor and those other two brains to show up.

It just wasn't right.

Even if she was a pain-in-the-ass.

Still, no matter how much I try, I can't seem to shake her. In fact, if you want to know the truth, she's even more of a

[143]

problem now than she ever was. Before, she just used to call me on the telephone. Now her brain follows me around, floating in and out of my head like fog or some bad dream.

It drives me crazy, even though I'm sure one of these days it'll all end and she'll go away and leave me in peace.

In the meantime, however, I guess I'll just have to be patient and keep on doing what I've been doing —slicing people's liverwurst and salami down at the General Store, bringing them their bowls of clam chowder and pea soup, and staying clear of the jar of pickled pigs feet.

TAKEN

Joanna H. Woś

*And they the ones that come bother you like that. Some-
times they come in and you hear them just walking. They
open the door and come in and come to your bed and jerk
your covers off, or either just pull your hair like that or
hold your hand. That's when they do that to you . . . twist
your face.*

Sanapia: Comanche Medicine Woman

My mother's hand made me cry this morning. Thinking of her hand, I mean. I had been up most of the night. My
little boy was sick. I held his hand, to help him fall asleep. When
I finally lay down, it was her hand I felt. I kept feeling her hand
in mine. Her hand had been soft and puffy, like my baby's.

When I was his age, I had my first nightmare. I was asleep
in a big bed, all by myself. I dreamt about a hand. The hand came
up from between the wall and the bed. The hand tried to take
me. My mother came to comfort me. She hugged me in her
arms. I did not know how to tell her about what had frightened
me.

I do not know how to tell about my mother's hand. I
already said her hand was soft and puffy. She wanted me to
hold her hand. I wanted to play. She wanted to hold my hand.
I wanted to go back outside. She closed her eyes and held my
hand. I let go of her hand, because I wanted to believe she was
asleep. My hand left an impression in her soft skin, like my
son's handprints in clay. She kept her eyes shut until I was
gone. I ran around the yard with the neighborhood kids. I saw
her look down from her bedroom window. I played tag in the
sun. A month later I wanted to hold her hand. Her hand was

hard and cold by then. When I touched her hand, my fingers left
no mark.

I have heard about a tribe that fears the hand that takes
you in the night.   The Comanche believe in ghost-sickness.
Once you are taken by the hand, you walk in the real world but
you do not see. Your face is frozen, twisted. You cannot feel the
wind.   Unless you atone for leaving the old ways, the hand
never lets you go and you are never healed. The only defense
against the ghost is courage. You cannot just glance at a ghost.
You must turn your whole body around and look right at it. You
must say, "Come here, let me see you." Before I had a son, I slept
with my hands beneath the covers.

We are going to visit my father this morning. The drive is
eight hours each way. Tomorrow is Thanksgiving. This time
when he repeats his same old stories, I will take his hand. As we
sit together, I will close my eyes. Maybe I will fall asleep. Or
maybe I will think about holding hands.

UNCONSCIOUS GIFTS
Excerpts From a Memorial Installation
In Honor of My Mother

Mary Jane Westbrook

Memory

When we released my mother's ashes I released her memory. The memory of her that had been bound by time. Now she is no longer bound by time and she is not bound by memory either. I am bound by memory because I am bound by time. Not bound in a restrictive sense. Just bound by the borders of my body.

I thought about keeping a handful of my mother's ashes when we scattered them at the duck pond. Just quietly slipping some into my pocket. Nobody would know. It would be my secret. A handful of my mother I could carry with me always. Then I thought what is Always? and I didn't do it. I didn't keep the ashes. I let them go, all of them, and I thought this is the most you can love somebody. It has more mostness to it than any way I have tried. Now I want to love living people that way too. With mostness. With releasing.

A friend of mine said memory lives in the body. In smells and touches.

Now I think my mother's ashes are memory ashes. They came in a box and I remember thinking they weren't very heavy. It was surprising to reach down into the plastic bag and pull out some gritty pieces that were actually recognizable as bones. A little finger or a toe bone. And I remembered the wig she had on because she lost all her hair and I remember asking the funeral director if the wig would be burned too and if she would be dressed in her pink dress and he said yes. So all of that was in there too and I added some wildflower seeds to the ashes so when we threw them out we threw out seed too. We threw them into the pond and along the shore and next to a couple of nests where some duck eggs were being guarded and warmed. We threw them into the air and sprinkled them around in the low growing trees and bushes. Into the slime that grew next to the shore and sometimes when we threw them into the air they came back on us and hit us in the face and we got ashes in our eyes.

Death

I am death and I am talking to you now. I've recently asked your mother to come and live with me. She agreed but not without a battle and a long one at that. The part of the struggle you saw lasted just under a year but it actually began long before that when she let go of her spirit. You know what I am talking about because the spirit she gave up went to you. It was her gift to you and she wanted you to have it but she was as ambivalent about giving her spirit away as she was about dying. She wanted to give her spirit to you but she wanted to keep it too, hold onto it for herself. Even if she did nothing with it, it was hers and no one could take it away. And her life, like her spirit, could only be given away with her permission, with her grace, with her authority. She fought with me about it and did everything she could to keep me from getting too close, and just when I had her almost within my embrace she handed her spirit gift over to you. You need to know this now because the conflict she had about giving it to you is getting in your way. Her ambivalence has become yours too. It came with the gift. Your mother's conflict was between using and squandering the gift. Yours is the struggle of protecting it and sharing it with other people. And since you have decided to accept this responsibility, from her release and in this struggle you will find the freedom of not disguising a gift that is there.

I had to convince your mother to come to me, to find another way to live. I almost had her at Thanksgiving last year. Just as I was rejoicing in the preparation I made for her arrival, she found some kind of strength to resist me. I was happy too soon, as I stood here waiting, rubbing my hands together and smiling an evil smile. My desire for her was so pure I was sure a gleam would bounce from my eyes as they grinned in presumptuous expectation. I am possession you see. I am not just death, the one that is absent and void. I am the possession which is relentlessly ungiving. Once you have known my embrace you know no other. Not the embrace of comfort. Not the embrace of a simple living. You will never know innocence again. Never will you know the birth of something without knowing it is death too, the possession of non-living. Never will you see a kitten without knowing how the loss of that kitten will feel. Never will you see your sister without knowing how the death of that sister will feel and never will you look at yourself in the mirror and not know how the loss of your own life will feel. And though the decision to release is an act of grace, my embrace is not. I am not graceful. I am awkward.

Birth

I don't know why we got her back in a cardboard box but we did. Maybe because we were going to release her ashes and not save them. Ron and I went to the funeral home to pick them up and when the man handed them to me I braced myself to hold a heavy weight. I thought they would weigh what my mother weighed when she died but they didn't. They must have weighed five or ten pounds maybe, but they didn't weigh eighty. Maybe it was her soul that weighed so much.

The box seemed so plain, a box I would go to the packaging store to buy, and such a contrast from the last time I saw my mother here where the dead lay their heads on satin pillows and the stairs going up to the viewing rooms are padded and puffy and the windows are draped to keep the everyday sunshine out. This is a separate world, a world that is not an everyday world. It is a time that is not an everyday time, but everyday time must be lived in, and death time too. Loss time. Everyday things must be done, and everyday things and death things are done together. It is a time of living in two times. A time of living in between and among, outside and inside.

A lonely time and a rich time. A time to inherit. To come into the possession of memory. To possess. To receive memory as a person. To possess and to receive what was not given in life. Her nurturing, her support, her power. Her validation, her acknowledgment, her recognition. Her needs, her wants. My needs, my wants.

And with her release she has twice given me birth. She has given me my needs, my wants, my power. This is my inheritance. This is my legacy. This is my birth.

THE PINK ROOM

Carolyn Weathers

Until Mother died, there was no such thing as the Pink Room. Jenny and I had only a spare room in our artists' loft. When I got back to Los Angeles, I put into this spare room all of Mother's things that I had brought back from Texas, stuffing into cardboard boxes and into the car leftovers of my mother — kindhearted Mother, the farmer's daughter, the softspoken and fair-minded woman who hated cruelty, who worried incessantly, who had a bottomless well of fortitude; who loved the Golden Rule, the Spanish language, clear thinking and creature comforts; who would rather make nice than make waves, and who all her life avoided risking ostracism because she feared ostracism more than death.

At first, Mother's things stayed piled in the hall while I painted the spare room pink — not the walls — but the floor, the woodwork, the door handles, the inside of the lock. I painted great pink waves rising up from the woodwork onto the lower walls. I painted the hall floor outside the Pink Room, as though tides of pink had rolled out.

The color pink had no significance to me other than that I liked it. What was significant was my pink abandon, frenzy of pink, like manic laughter, like the frenzied laughter when my aunt, my sister and I were sitting in my dying mother's hospital room and we sheepishly realized we had the munchies, and we weren't sure, any of us, that that was okay. But the fact was, we did have the munchies, so my sister and I went on a junk food run and brought back to the hospital room bags of Fritoes and Twinkies, Slurpies and microwave burritos, which we eagerly tore into and consumed, while three feet away my mother lay in a coma on her last night on earth. Pink, laughing frenzy, like when our favorite nurse interrupted our picnic to do a suction on Mother and we all three jumped up and headed for the door, telling the nurse we weren't about to stay around for that disgusting procedure. "Well, really," I said. "We'll just take our food and go!" And we sashayed out, shrieking with hilarity.

Hysterical pink, rising in comical waves up from the woodwork and out into the hall.

When the paint was dry, I bought ten metal shelves. Hour after hour, I sat on the pink floor, fastening metal shelves together with nuts and bolts. I stood the assembled shelves all around the walls of the Pink Room, then moved Mother's things in from the hall.

Into the Pink Room went the wind chimes, the wooden spirals that turned in the wind, the faded artificial grapes and plums.

Into the corners went three garbage sacks of Mother's clothes. Onto the shelves went Mother's jewelry boxes overflowing with bracelets, necklaces, pins, fake pearls, old-fashioned earscrews and the many earrings she enjoyed wearing after she had her ears pierced when she was seventy.

Onto the shelves went her candy dish with cherubs dancing around the stem, her piggy bank with coins still sliding around inside, her sewing basket full of old letters, dating from when she lived in California, living the life of a World War II Army chaplain's wife with two small daughters. Beside her sewing basket, went a shoebox stuffed with baby clothes that had belonged to my sister and me and which my mother had kept all those forty-eight years.

Her beat-up Scrabble set, her dominos.

Her algebra book. She used to work algebra for fun, while my awed, poetic father and I struggled along with our copy of *Everyday Mathematics for the Common Man*.

Beside her algebra book, I propped relics from her days as a high school teacher — her English and Spanish textbooks. She had loved teaching grammar and could make diagramming sentences almost seem exciting, but she hated teaching literature, not because she hated literature, but because she was so bored with teaching *Julius Caesar* year after year, she could have run him through with a dagger herself.

Julius came to rest, with the textbooks, next to a box of old photographs. My eighteen year old mother smiled up at me in her flapper haircut and Waco High School letter sweater. She won the letter in basketball. In high school and later with the Texas Amateur Athletic Association, she was a star forward, putting her whole heart into burning up the courts and making baskets.

I closed the lid over Mother's photograph and set the box on a shelf beside her college diploma. She had graduated magna cum laude at the age of fifty and received tumultuous applause as she strode head-up across the stage, with her smile and prematurely gray hair shining. My father was so proud of her. That was 1960, and the next year he died.

Around the Pink Room I went with my treasures, filling up the metal shelves. I lugged in Mother's Big Band records and fondly remembered how she had come to like the Mamas and the Papas almost as much as Tommy Dorsey. I stacked the Big Band records against the wall, where they stood, testimonies to the Baptist preacher's wife who secretly loved to dance, who taught me to Charleston and who laughed so hard when I taught her how to do the Twist.

When I came to her cordless phone, it never entered my head to actually use it. Something inside urged me to set it on a shelf, and I did. The cordless phone was the last gift I ever gave my mother, bought for her when she got too weak to get to her wall phone, and she was endlessly thrilled and grateful, as though I'd given her a candy store.

Onto the shelves went her microwave and her portable cassette recorder. Still taped to the cassette recorder were the notes I had hand-printed in large, dark letters so that Mother, whose eyes had gone bad years earlier, could see how to work it. *Play, Stop, Rewind* and *Fast Forward* read the notes, all with my hand-drawn arrows pointing in the appropriate directions to move the button. The notes were of no use now, but I couldn't bring myself to peel them off. The notes would stay taped to the cassette recorder, the cassette recorder would stay on the shelf with the cordless phone, microwave, the sheets, towels and blankets, the overflowing jewelry boxes and sacks of clothes, all of them rendered into statuary, distant from their practical purposes. Distant like museums, shrines, like the dead.

Onto the wall went Mother's long kitchen calendar, the one made of coarse cloth with geese marching across the top of it, marking a year that was forever 1988, marking a memory forever burned in my brain of Mother and me trying to coordinate the best time for my sister's partner, Vicki in Seattle, and mine, Jenny in Los Angeles, to visit so we could all have Christmas together — of how Christmas was moved up to the first of November, the first of November to as quickly as possible — of how Mother died two days before Jenny and Vicki could get there.

The Pink Room was filling, but it could never be so filled that it took away from the pinkness. Pink, like Mother's many pink queer friends back in California, whom she had loved and who loved her, whose flowers had stood ironically juxtaposed around the funeral home with flowers sent by her church and senior center friends in Texas, friends who never dreamed that queers had mothers, who never knew that Mother was paralyzed with fear they should find out that her own daughters, whom they thought so fine, were queers. She could not bear to imagine any of us ostracized. For years, my sister and I had urged Mother to tell her sister about us, assuring her that in Auntie Fae she would find an ally in the Bible Belt, but she couldn't. After Mother's funeral, I told Auntie Fae we were gay, and she said that's what she'd figured all along, and she loved us just the same anyway. She said she'd given Mother many opportunities through the years to tell her. We had had to see Mother's body to the grave before we could share her terrible and unnecessary secret.

Shocking pink everywhere, even where least expected, in the keyhole, on the floor.

Into an outlet I plugged the night light, Mother's first and last one, which she kept lit during the last months of her life. I turned it on, and all Mother's objects, all the love and sadness, all my sense of connection to her, seemed manifested in that small and vigilant glow. "Go to the light," my sister and I had whispered over and over to our mother during her last day, after she slipped into a morphine drip- and cancer- coma but before she slipped down past the point of hearing. We whispered that she was terrific, that she had given us so much of value, that everyone who knew her said she brought good into their lives; that she did great. We told her that she didn't have to worry about us, that it was okay to go. "We'll always love you," we whispered, "and the light loves you, too."

In the Pink Room, I kept the night light on both day and night.

Near the night light I hung a framed photograph of Mother taken three months before her death. She had had it made, knowing she would soon die, to give to her loved ones. In the photograph, she looked kindly, and still beautiful at seventy-eight; she smiled gently, almost tentatively. The Pink Room was painted the same hot pink as the blouse she wore.

The Pink Room was complete now.

I felt comforted when I went in there and sat in the chair, put my feet up on the hassock, turned on three lights of the pole lamp, just like Mother used to do, and wrote in my journal. Sometimes, a breeze would blow through the window, causing the revolving wooden spirals to move and the wind chimes to ting-ting. The first time it happened, I said out loud, "Mother?" But, of course, it was the breeze.

Even though I felt Mother's absence and not her presence, sitting in the Pink Room calmed me and made me feel close to her. Contrasting feelings swirled inside me — high stress, the pain of loss, a strange calm and a powerful detachment. The Pink Room cushioned me while Mother's death sunk in, cushioning me like food, like the forty pounds I gained in the months preceding and following her death, pounds that felt like a sturdy fortress around me. How soothing it felt to be a plump woman in midlife, savoring, as she passed through the natural and benign life cycle, her frozen Margaritas, those enchiladas, that pecan pie and chocolate sundae. Reality was simple, where once it had been complex — now it was food and drink and the indulging in them; solid, comfortable basics; concrete and practical tasks. I was freed from my addictive urge to ask the Big Questions, to think about the meaning of life and death, the horror of suffering, human and animal.

Sitting in the Pink Room, I felt that Mother, my aunt, my sister and Vicki, Jenny and I were being carried off by Enormity, like we were part of something huge and hallowed, and we were as out of control in it as atoms in the Big Bang.

I felt a sweet peace, a bittersweet loss. Mother was so

benign, she made death seem benign. Yet even as I soaked in a benign sea, I felt sad, untethered and wild. Desperation raged beneath the plump gourmand.

The Pink Room — cocoon room, womb room, was my homemade harbor.

As the months passed, the shock of Mother's death and the feeling of being lifted out of everyday life melted away. Hallowed and benign Enormity dissolved, nibbled up by daily life. I loved Mother as much as ever, but I had come closer to unifying her death in equal parts in my memory with Mother's whole self. As my protective detachment wore off, so did the cushioning effect of the forty extra pounds. Gluttonizing my way through the life cycle didn't soothe me anymore. I bought a Nordic Track cross-country ski machine, determined to strenuously burn fat into muscle.

Gradually, the Pink Room faded in importance. I stopped sitting in the chair, started moving objects into the Pink Room unrelated to Mother and her death. I began to take Mother's things and incorporate them into the rest of the loft. I put her microwave in the kitchen, her blankets on the bed. I hung her wind chimes in a window, her artificial grapes and plums over the bar. I started wearing Mother's jewelry, using her cordless phone, playing tapes in her cassette recorder, cooking with her microwave. I hung her photograph in my busy writing room. I started thinking about life, death and the horror of suffering.

Everyday, Mother haunted my mind. She still does.

A year after Mother died, Jenny and I painted the Pink Room white and rented it out.

••••

————— **INHERITANCE** —————

NETTA E.

Hermine Pinson

When I hear somebody like Charles Earland stroking *Never Knew Love Like This Before*, or Bill Evans' poignant piano on *You Must Believe in Spring*, I know that hers was not a simple despair, but a hard-won peace that she negotiated with God and herself. Because beyond the word is music, the word taken flight, the word set free from making sense, from being explicit. And that is Mama, in the middle of the floor on Ruth Street, showing us how to dance free-style, "choi cha choi chop choi — ah bop ah bop ah bop" — contrapuntal patter, soul-clapping dance to make the weary floorboards of Mr. Lovell's renthouse creak in accompaniment. When did I release her, or that part of her that was in pain, give it away to Ochun's fecund earth, to Oya's wind? Long time coming. Mama . . . .

Was naive, intelligent, sensitive, intense, suspicious and finally dangerous. Yet, she brought me, my brother and sister through before she turned back and gave what was left of herself to despair. Mama . . . I can hear her fluent alto, *We are climbing Jacob's ladder/ Every round goes higher, higher,* as she vainly scrubs the yellowed bathtub on Ruth Street. The tiny house with its spacious backyard, where Mama grew grapes that she made into jelly, is gone now, just like Mama is gone. Ruth Street yielded to a new freeway; Mama, August's child, yielded to the fire she had always feared would come and get her, much like the fire that had wrapped its flames around her preacher-father's house when she was seventeen.

There are nights when I blame her for dying, when I blame her for letting her cigarette slip from her hands onto the car-peted floor. The fire had already begun to eat its way to the living room by the time she woke, coughing and gasping. She crawled as far as the front door of the tiny apartment she occupied on Kelsey Street, where she had moved to sort out the wheat from the chaff of her life with us.

My father arrived home early that morning. He'd been out all night letting Alvia Walker pretend she was his wife. The chill in the air was alien to heat-laden August. He went from room to room, waking me, Nadine and Cooper to say that there had been a fire and Mama had died of smoke inhalation. When we were all gathered in the living room, he quietly told us what had happened.

I had never really talked to my father, because I was afraid of his anger and angry at the authority he took for granted. Like Mama, Daddy was an only child, but unlike Mama, he always started and ended with his particular angle on the universe. There was his way or no way. He often told us, "We can sit down and discuss the big decisions, where to move next, whether to move or buy a car, but I will make the final decision." His "I" was the only one that counted.

But this August morning, I answered his account, saying, "You're lying," My brother and sister hid their own reactions behind blank stares as I leaped up from the couch where they sat like two blackbirds on a plaid bough and strode to my room, as if getting into bed and closing my eyes would prove that this was just a dream. Following me to my room, Daddy gently touched my shoulder. "Baby, you've got to get up. We're going to the apartment to get your mother's things."

"Things? What things? Didn't you say she was in a fire? What was saved? How do you know all this?" The words rushed out, dry autumnal leaves blown by some malevolent wind.

My father was not a mean man. I simply could not talk to him. When Cooper Ezekiel Hayden, Sr. asked you a question, you answered within one beat of the question, otherwise he'd accuse you of procrastinating. "Well, hell, get it out, girl! What are you trying to say? Did you pass the history test or not?" He interpreted delay as equivocation. So I usually stayed my distance. I had learned at the age of eight that the best way to avoid my father's contempt or ridicule was to hide behind a book. He liked to see you reading; that meant you were accomplishing something, or maybe it meant that there was one less voice for him to contend with for a while. He so loved to talk. He was words, and Mama was music. He was Shango's thunder; Mama was Oya's mellifluous windchimes, when she wanted to be, ordering random noise, urban cacophony into meaning, whether she played it herself on our upright piano or brought it to us in stereo — Bach's concerto, Ellington's suite.

As a lawyer's wife and a woman who had been out of school for at least twenty years, Mama had few resources of her own, maybe a credit card that said *Mrs. Cooper E. Hayden.* And she'd been to Ross Psychiatric Hospital twice for "nervous exhaustion," or at least that's what Daddy told inquiring friends and Mama's relatives.

That's what he told us, his children, as we packed her bags for another trip to the laughing academy, while Mama sat quietly in the living room, next to an ashtray brimming with cigarette butts, the only sign of her apprehension. Who would allow such a woman to have custody of three children? Who would plead her case for her? Would the doctors' and lawyers' wives who had made a precarious peace with their own lives risk discomfort for one eccentric sister whose penchant for Basie, Brubeck and bourbon disqualified her to play "nigger bridge" and aimlessly shop at Neiman Marcus? "Not hardly," Mama would say of her women acquaintances.

When we'd arrived in Houston from Nashville, Mama attended one bridge session, denounced the whole cadre of permanent waves, and determined that she was her own best company. Her piano, her whiskey, and her memories were infinitely more interesting than the price of a new dress or the impertinence of a black maid. Unwilling to learn new names and new assimilationist games, she called no one, and after a while no one called her.

We, Mama's children, had our own way of coping. Like the typical "dysfunctional" family, there was the martyr (Nadine), the clown (me), the scapegoat (Coop, Jr.), the lost soul[s] (me, Nadine and Coop). Of course, we traded roles whenever the occasion arose. I'd try to distract Mama from going out of the house to Baldy Plump's Bar & Grill where she'd sit until she passed out and one of her drinkin' buddies would drive her home. Either I'd get her to talk about accomplishments of her illustrious Richmond siblings and how her mother's brilliant brother, Robert, was still somewhere in Zaire doing nation-building with his architectural skills; or, if she was in the grip of delirium tremens, I'd act out the drama with her, asking her to show me where the little red men were coming in through the crack in the roof. Often too tired to put up with Mama's foolishness, Nadine would retire to her room after writing out bills or answering the calls of curious aunts, grandmothers and distant uncles who missed Mama's delightful letters. Mama was the family historian and communicator. But after a while she lost interest in doing anything that took her mind off her own deterioration and her husband's growing indifference. Cooper, Jr., was often encouraged to play with the next-door neighbor's child or sent to spend the night with Miss Nash's happy, boisterous family.

One spring, after an especially lengthy stay at Ross, Mama came home a quiet, sober, determined woman. She waited until Coop went off on one of his "business" trips with Alvia to make her move. Tired of being mistaken for the truly crazy, tired of being misinterpreted by misogynist male psychiatrists, Mama used Coop's credit cards to find herself a place to be. She moved to a one-bedroom apartment on Kelsey Street near the Astrodome; she just up and moved. Didn't even give us a key to her apartment, although she did give us her phone number and sometimes called when she was lonely or she'd fallen off the wagon. Mama had a habit of lighting a cigarette in one room, placing it in an ashtray and lighting another one in another room. When she was living at home, it wasn't a problem because Mrs. Nash, the housekeeper, was always there to put out Mama's cigarettes or take the cigarette to her. Although taking care of Mama was not in Mrs. Nash's job description, that is why she had been hired. She had the unpleasant duty of playing a game with Mama called "hide the bourbon."

Daddy had given Mrs. Nash strict instructions not to allow Mama to drink anything stronger than coffee and soda. But Mama always managed to find the bottle, no matter where Mrs. Nash hid it. Once, Mrs. Nash stashed the bottle in the washing machine and forgot to take it out when she put the clothes in. Everybody's underwear smelled like Jack Daniels (Black Label) and the repair man carted away the washing machine. By ninth grade Nadine and I would alternate staying at home on Mondays to take care of Coop, Jr. because Mrs. Nash didn't come to work on Sundays and Mondays. If somebody didn't stay at home, Coop, Jr. would be out in front of the house, building dirt castles in his dirty diaper, happily unencumbered by neither shirt nor shoes. Mama would be in the den, in the same chair we'd left her that morning, "asleep," as she called it. The sour odor of alcohol and cigarettes rose and fell with her breathing, bubbling at the corners of her lips as she fitfully snored. Carmen McRea's *Spring is Here* mocking itself, stuck in the rut of a scratch that had deepened with time and much use.

Mama had never been one to reveal her unadorned emotions to her children. That would not do for a woman whose Presbyterian minister father had first preached, then beaten stoicism into his only child. She never confided in her children. Even after she had given herself over to a blues that haunted her mornings and evenings, she still reigned supreme in her household, albeit haphazardly, Pall Mall in one hand, whiskey tumbler in the other, her brocade dressing gown trailing behind her. "Don't dispute me!" were her favorite words if she even thought you were forgetting who was in charge. "Girl, I'll slap your head off and glue it back on again!" she'd declare in her cigarette-and-whiskey-cured alto.

She had made us out of the blood, muscle and bones of her own body, taught us what we knew of poetry, music and dance. Even if the other little fifth graders didn't know who Paul Robeson was or why Billie Holiday sang the blues, we did. "Sit down and watch. This is important. Do you know why Leonard Bernstein moves his hands this way? It's four-four time;" and we'd duly take account of the proud Jewish maestro on Sunday evenings when Billy Sweet and Mrs. Johnson's twins were outside getting in the last game of kickball before they straggled home.

We arrived at the apartment on Kelsey Street by seven. The tranquilizer I had stuffed in my mouth before leaving the house had taken effect quickly. I waded through the black charred debris in a Valium daze. I'd discovered the wonders of the tiny pills one night when Daddy told me to bring him one from the medicine cabinet. Curious about the powerful effects of this little pill that made Daddy so calm in the face of the domestic chaos he often found when he dragged home from work or play, I'd stolen one for myself. Thereafter, I'd take one whenever I didn't want to feel, whenever I wanted to wrap myself in the warm blanket of numb.

[163]

The morning of the funeral Daddy knew I was the one who would probably shatter the decorum of the service, shred the false tranquility of John Calvin Presbyterian Church with my loud, bitter grief. And Coop Hayden, Sr. was not going to allow one hysterical twenty-year old woman make him or his family look bad. He went into the medicine cabinet and got me two Triavils. I took both pills, washing them down with a shot of Mama's favorite bourbon, Jack Daniels Black Label. I sealed the memory of the funeral way down deep where it could neither haunt nor heal me. For sixteen years I would not return to the cemetery for a visit. Every year on Mother's Day I promised myself that I would go. Every year I'd spent the day in bed. And so I'd let the years pile up like miles on the highway. Mother's Day, 1985, spring had already greened a city hard-pressed by summer to commit to interminably blue skies.

I know the way, as I drive the ten miles outside the city limits. I don't want to think about Mama, but she touches my memory like she once touched the keys of our old upright piano. I see flash-photos of a grubby, honest street in Nashville. Mama's young again, her thick black hair barely contained by a ponytail. She's wearing a Hawaiian shirt over pink pedal-pushers. Wild yellow flowers move on her shoulders as she irons shirts after pants after blouses. She has a cigarette clamped to the side of her mouth, one eye squinched up, smoke and steam filling up the tiny dining room. Sweat beads her nose, as one shirt after another yields its wrinkles and creases to her will.

Where is she among the seemingly infinite flat stones that carpet the cemetery? I should know where she is, but I can't find her grave. She's not here in the shade of the pecan tree where she ought to be resting, after having borne three children as well as equal parts of Cooper Hayden's joy, affection and wrath for over twenty years.

Stumbling in memory's ample and quixotic storeroom, I've forgotten where I am and what I'm looking for. I feel myself drifting toward a familiar blues, a Quaalude despair. I think it is my heart beating, but I can feel the rhythm under my feet. Peering over the high hedge that separates the cemetery from the rest of the world, I find myself standing squarely in front of Vernell's Icehouse. Pickup trucks, women in deviously designed jeans and men in cowboy boots amble in and out, the music following them to their cars and out onto the wide highway. Who is that — Dinah Washington? Sounds like, no, that's Etta James blues. Toe-tappin' boogie has rudely collided with the attic-silence of memory. I crane my neck to see better. *Nobody loves me but my mama, and she could be jivin' too.* A wide-hipped woman in a bright-tight print dress and well-worn cowboy boots leans on a Chevy pickup, giving and taking sweet talk, promises and lies. "The joint is live!" as Coop would say.

Tripping over the stone and bronze obstacles, I move closer to the music. I don't know why I look down when I do, but right there, just two feet from the hedges and fifty feet from the front door of Vernell's, there it is: *In loving memory of Netta Elaine Richmond Hayden (1934-1969)* and right next to her plaque with its Delta Sigma Theta insignia is Coop's plaque, just his name and his date of birth. My face doesn't know which way to go, so it goes several ways at once. Tears fill the part of my eyes that aren't beginning to laugh; trembling lips let go and smile. She's not here, and she never was here where my memory has left her to lie these many years. I think of Sister Caroline of James Weldon Johnson's *Go Down Death.* Like her, Mama has gone home. I am a part of what she left, Nadine and Coop Jr., me and my children. We are her legacy and her gift to this weird, wonderful world.

I cannot believe I am patting my foot to B. B. King at the side of my mother's grave. I should have known Mama's grave would be where there was music and laughter and living. There is nothing to say, nothing to do except nod my head to the dependable bass line of B. B.'s riff, to soak up the rutted grooves of B. B.'s sweet vibrato, to be here inside the moment, inside the music, being held, being carried in rhythm's cradle. Because if I'd wanted a seance to call back the departed, this is the place to improvise a meeting, and we do, me, Mama and B. B.

A slow grin gives way to a smile to a gentle chuckle. What have I feared, why have I feared? In answer, Curtis Mayfield clears his throat just in time to sing *'Cause it's all right, it's all right, have a good time, 'cause it's all right.* Fire and despair have no power here. Mama is here and she's not here — she's music and that part of my soul that remembers to sing.

And it's all right.

FINDING HOME

Karen Kandik

Not long after my mother died I realized I was mildly surprised that I was still alive and had not died with her. It was not that I had ever consciously thought that I would die if my mother did; I had just never thought of life without her. I had even envisioned my mother's death for fleeting moments when I heard of others' mothers dying. I would shudder and move quickly into the intellectual realm of "How sad for that woman." But I had never imagined how it would feel to actually have my own mother die. I had envisioned her death but not life after her death.

It is a law of physics that there are no natural vacuums. It did not feel that way after my mother died. I felt empty, numb, like my insides were being sucked out as soon as something was there to fill them. I functioned in my daily life; I went to work, saw friends, did routine activities. Whenever I would feel like crying, it didn't seem to be at an "appropriate" time. On the way to work? Red eyes raise eyebrows. At night before sleeping? Not bad but then one awoke tired the next day. Certainly not with others; they would be embarrassed and confused and I would probably end up taking care of them. By not grieving more openly, I now feel that I prolonged the healing and drove it underground.

At the time, however, I did not know that there are no "rules" to grieving. I knew the stages of grief and was anxious to get through them all so that I wouldn't hurt anymore; I would be back to normal. I was assured that it was "normal" to grieve for a long time. I didn't feel normal. I felt like screaming "I will NEVER be normal. My MOTHER is dead." Gradually, I have come to realize that being without a mother is what is "normal" for me; my world has shifted noticeably to a different "normality".

I still find that my sorrow happens at odd moments; when I can't do something, usually mechanical, that I know my mother could have done; when I see a piece of orange fabric — the sheer sensuality of which she would have enjoyed. I used to think it strange to react like that; now I accept it as "normal," as I get older and accept myself as "normal" and learn to fill up the vacuum by myself, as much as one person can.

Other parts of the vacuum have been filled by surprising sources. My father, with whom I had never been particularly close, has gradually become more important to me. I am seeing the nurturing, sensitive side of him and even allow him to take care of me emotionally at times. My best friend's mother told me that I can be her "other daughter." My mother's sister and I have since shared many laughs and heart-to-heart talks even though she lives far away. My father's new wife wisely has never tried to be my stepmother but has enjoyed getting to know me as a friend. A remarkable ninety-six-year-old woman took me into her confidence and shared her enthusiasm, intelligence, philosophies and ideals. She reminded me so much of my mother that her death affected me nearly as much.

There was a "Peanuts" cartoon which I had saved from my college days. Charlie Brown talks about being in the back seat of a car at night with his mom and dad driving home. That cartoon conjured up safe thoughts and comforting images for me. The cartoon ends with Charlie Brown pointing out that, of course, this doesn't last, that you grow up and never get to sleep in the back seat again. That is how I felt when my mom died; I could never again sleep in the back seat. I had to be in the driver's seat.

My mother stressed independence in her children and modeled that trait well. But I never really knew until after she died that being independent doesn't mean that you cannot rely on other people. I had to learn that fact after she died and I couldn't fill up the vacuum alone. There will always be a hole that will never be filled but it doesn't mean that I feel so empty anymore.

My mother gave me few guideposts when she was living for how to deal with her dying. Or maybe I just wasn't paying enough attention. It has been a struggle to accept, remember, and feel those clues which she did leave behind. I felt ill-prepared and on quicksand from the minute of her diagnosis with cancer to some point, years later, when I no longer ques-

[167]

tioned why I was crying at certain times; I just knew.

Even though I was fifteen when my maternal grandmother died, I have absolutely no recollection of how my mother reacted to her death. I remember it was a Sunday around noon when the call came from my uncle that my grandmother had died suddenly of a heart attack. I remember nothing after that. My mother went back to Ohio; I do not remember her leaving, her absence, or her return. In fact, though I learned from my aunt in later years that Mom and her mother had been very close, it was with difficulty that I remembered my mother ever talking about her mother again. I attributed that to my poor memory (which I do not have) until I asked my father recently what he could tell me about Mom's reaction to Grandma's death. He couldn't tell me anything.

There were three exceptions to the silence. One occurred when I was about eighteen years old. I was home from college and sitting in my room trying not to hear my parents argue — something that they rarely did so it was all the more disturbing to me. Not long after the talking ended, my mother came into my room crying. I felt quite uncomfortable seeing her stand and look out the window; I could count on one hand the number of times that I had seen her cry. She didn't speak to me, just looked out the window and sobbed, "Sometimes I miss my mother so much." I was scared, startled, embarrassed. But I never forgot that incident; in fact, I have clung to it as "proof" that it is all right to grieve for your mother years after her death. The second exception occurred years later when she became ill. When my mother's cancer was first diagnosed, she had surgery, which was supposed to "cure" it. She told me that she was sure that she was going to be fine, that she wasn't going to allow herself to think anything else. I lived with that hope for the next eight months in spite of researching the illness myself and learning only bleak information, in spite of the visible evidence that her health was declining rapidly, in spite of her being told that the cancer had spread to many parts of her body. No one told me that she was dying and so, therefore, she wasn't. My father and one of her doctors kept talking about this or that new drug and when she would go home. I made plans, internally, to take time off from work and help her recuperate. I went with her to physical therapy and saw how she could not write her name or walk more than a few halting steps — but she was going to get better. No one told me that she wasn't. Until her other doctor spoke to my dad and me one cold February afternoon and spoke in terms of "days or months." I recall my father sitting there very calmly in this man's office and nodding his head: I was incredulous. Die? My mother was going to die? Surely it was a mistake. But no, this doctor who seemed to know what he was talking about and my father, an honorable man who didn't lie, were accepting this like it was really going to happen. The doctor left his office and my father and I started back to my mother's room. In the middle of the hallway, I burst into tears and threw my arms around my father's neck, something that startled both of us. We went back into the office and I sobbed as my father, trying his best to cope with the same knowledge about the woman he loved more than anyone in the world, gently told me that this doctor was a pessimist, that her other doctor was more hopeful and that we must not tell Mom about this because it would only set her back in her recovery. I became the little girl and acquiesced.

When we got back to Mom's room, I picked up my knitting and sat by her bedside. It was hard to retain my composure; I kept sniffing, ready to explode at any moment. My mother, her eyes closed, said to me, "Do you have a cold?" I responded, truthfully, "No." She opened her eyes at that point — a great effort — and said, "I lost my mother when I was forty-one. It takes a while but you get over it." Then she closed her eyes again and resumed her drug-induced serenity. I left the hospital and went home to my childhood room and screamed until I was hoarse. The doctors had made it real and oh, God, so had my mother. The fact that I would "get over it" was no consolation at that point. It became consolation after her death when I seriously wondered if the pain would ever lessen.

The third exception occurred after my mother died. I had a dream so vivid that I remember it clearly eight years later:

I, as an adult, am sitting on the front steps of the house where I grew up. My mother is sitting one step up from me and I am tucked in between her legs. She is leaning over and has her arms around me. And all she says is, "It's going to be all right."

When I awoke, I thought it was to her touch and the sound of her voice. I think of it as her final gift to me.

MY MOTHER, MY JOAN

Carol Anne Douglas

When I first saw a Katharine Hepburn movie, Hepburn's bearing, dignity, intelligence and liveliness reminded me of my mother. Even though my mother was married and had a child, the idea of her being some man's sex object was simply ridiculous. She had too much dignity to be easily imagined in that role.

But there she was, unable to remember her name, not knowing where she was, frustrated if you asked her questions, still able to perceive that she didn't know the answers and to be embarrassed. At first, she tried to fake it, to say "yes" and "no" and hope she said them in the right place.

Layer after layer of words and customs slipped, leaving only Joan, the emotions. She lost the ability to count. "Two thousand dollars?" she asked the clerk in the drug store regarding the price of hairpins. She lost the ability to dial a telephone, turn on a television, or cook. She remembered how to turn the stove on, but never turned it off.

Eventually, the words peeled away — the prepositions, the nouns, the verbs. A few phrases remained, "It's beautiful," "That's good," "That's awful," "Let's go," and "I love you," and, of course, "No."

Alzheimer's disease took my mother ten years before death did. It took her and left me with Joan, a frightened girl-woman. I had her live with me for four months, and I never had a night's sleep. She was up during the night, with her coat on, wanting to go out shopping. She turned the light on in my face and said, "Let's go out," and I tried to explain that it was 2:00 a.m., no stores were open, and she should go back to bed. "We can't go?" she would say, tragically, and cry. Finally, I would get her back to bed.

Then she would wake me up at 4:00 a.m. and tell me that a lot of boys and girls were coming to dinner and she had the meal ready. I would get up and find our food for the week wrecked in the oven.

I felt that I could not continue, as a single lesbian scraping by in a one-bedroom apartment and going to work each day, to take care of her — yet she had coped with my waking her up in the middle of the night when I was a baby. I called every retirement home in the Washington, D.C. area and found that none of them would take a woman who was, as they euphemistically said, "confused."

I toured nursing homes, trying to find one that would be humanly possible for her to live in. I smelled the smells. I learned that the ones where confused-looking people wandered around were the better ones — the patients were not tied down. I learned that there are better and worse levels of hell, as Dante described, and tried to find one of the better hells for my mother.

There was nothing for her to buy at the nursing home, but I gave her a purse and some money because she wanted to feel that she had some. (I had become her guardian and was managing her money, ashamed every time I wrote a check to the nursing home or doctor because I had seen so many television shows that stereotypically portrayed the evil children trying to declare their parents incompetent and take their money.)

My teeth had gotten bad from years of skimping on visits to the dentist. One day, my mother handed me a little roll wrapped in Kleenex of one dollar bills that she'd been saving from the pocket money I gave her and pointed to my teeth. She wanted me to go to dentist. I will never remember any other gift she gave me without remembering the wad of bills, the gift she gave me from the nursing home. It was even better than the doll house, better than the garnet ring she could barely afford that was in my Christmas stocking when I was eighteen.

How is it possible to look back on your childhood and be happy about even the best memories when you know that the dearest person in them spent her last ten years in nursing homes? How can I remember anything—how we sat and talked at the kitchen table after she brought me home from school every day — without remembering her alone in a nursing home room and afraid? How can I remember how when I was little I used to beg her not to leave me at school, and stayed in her car as long as I could, not because I didn't like school but because I hated to be away from her all day? A few times I actually persuaded her to say I was sick and take me home with her. Then when she asked me to take her away from the nursing home to live with me, I couldn't. I tried to explain that although the nursing home was difficult it was the best one I could find (of course she never saw the bad ones) and I was sorry. And I left her.

If I had been the one who was stricken, she would have visited every day, not once a week as I visited her. I was always, always conscious that she would have visited me every day, as she had visited my father every day when he was in the hospital and nursing homes after a stroke. He cursed her and she came home and drank herself into oblivion. I wouldn't go after awhile because I wouldn't listen to the things he said about her (his delusion that she was plotting to lock him up) and I begged her not to go. She went.

My lesbian and feminist friends came with me to visit her, they accepted her into their homes for Thanksgiving and Christmas celebrations although she was a difficult guest, sometimes happy, sometimes confused and crying. She came to accept them and love some of them, she who would probably have refused to go to their homes or at least been very uncomfortable if she had been in her "normal" state.

How can I remember the Christmases of my childhood, the good, the less good, without remembering bringing Joan from the nursing home for Christmas celebrations — and bringing her back afterwards? I feel best about her first Christmas away from the nursing home, when we took her to a friend's home with a big tree, and she looked at it with eyes wide like a child's and said, "It's beautiful!" When we brought out the presents, she was astonished at how many were for her. "All of these are for me?" I felt at that moment as if she were my daughter, as well as my mother.

Her condition would last for awhile on a sort of plateau and then drop to a worse state. The pattern was repeated again and again.

After about six years, she became so dim that visits hardly seemed to bring her a moment of happiness. She didn't look at the flowers I brought or eat the cookies. She didn't register any pleasure at my presence. Nothing seemed to help. On the advice of friends, I drastically cut back on the visits. They made me hysterical — I would hyperventilate as soon as I left the floor where her room was — and didn't appear to help her. I don't know whether I did the right thing. I fear that during the years when I didn't visit much she had clearer spells that I missed.

She died the night before her seventy-eighth birthday. I thought, "What a good present for her." At last I knew that she was neither lonely, frightened, in pain nor abysmally bored.

I have always dreamed about her, but for many years I dreamed only of the Alzheimer's disease Joan, not of my mother before the Alzheimer's. Now, I dream of her as her old self. I always feel that each dream is a gift from her, almost like a visit.

I want her. How is it possible not to want your mother? How is it possible not to miss her love?

I find myself using expressions that she used, like, "Too much of a muchness," "That gives me the heebie-jeebies," or , "I'll give it a lick and a promise" (I'll clean it just a bit.). They pop into my head. I'm making a list of them.

Sometimes when I am alone, in the bathtub, or waking up in the middle of the night, I call out, "Mommy, Mommy." It is not entirely an innocent cry — I am immediately reminded of the people in nursing homes who call out ceaselessly, spasmodically — so crying out spontaneously is frightening to me, like a sign of madness.

When my mother died, I wanted to change my name to her maiden name, Joan Flannery. I wanted to have a daughter and name her "Joan." But how could I tell her her grandmother spent ten years in nursing homes? I did neither of these things — I know that I just wanted desperately for there to be a Joan — her — in the world.

I try to tell myself that I preserved her in preserving and developing the person she loved most — myself — but that seems awfully self-serving.

When I am successful at work, when I am pleasant but dignified and unflattering with a boss, I am being like her as she was before she married and when she worked after my father died. When I am being thoughtful to a woman, I am being like her.

In many ways, I am different from her. She rarely read,

and when she did, it was mysteries or historical romances. Reading and writing are central to my life. I disappointed her by not being athletic, as she had been as a child and young woman.

When I knew her, her major exercise, other than housework, was walking around the suburban block where we lived. I remember her eagerness to get out of the nursing home, how happy she was when I took her to see the cherry blossoms or some garden. Even after she broke her hip and was in a wheelchair, I tried to wheel her around the nursing home garden, but she was no longer very interested; she had been through too much to be placated with zinnias.

As she became more confined, I could no longer bear to be shut up in an office forty hours a week. I walk now more than I ever have before. I walk and walk in the woods. I walk, I walk, I will not be confined. I hope I somehow carry Joan with me. My eyes were a gift from her — they resemble her eyes. They are not her eyes, but they are nevertheless the eyes closest to hers.

We did much together, my mother and I — we baked cookies, we went out to dinner and the movies, to museums, always doing whatever I wanted. It was so hard to get an opinion on what she wanted. We went to Yosemite, we went to Mexico. The trips were the best because she managed not to drink when we were traveling.

I am not sure I could ever have torn myself away from her and started my own life if she hadn't drunk, if she had always been the perfect mother. She wanted so much to be a companion to me that I felt guilty about wanting a lover.

She was so irreverent for one so sweet — she was always perfectly polite to everyone, but we laughed about their foibles, whoever they were, clergy included. She was so sweet for one so irreverent — she gave everything anyone ever asked of her, except when I asked her to join Alcoholics Anonymous. She gave and gave like an endless cornucopia, money, attention, and time, more than she had. If another child's mother was sick, she drove her to school. If one of her nephews doing his years in the army gambled away his pay, he knew Aunt Joan was the one who would give him enough for the rest of the month and not tell his parents.

I want to be just like her; I don't want to be like her at all.

She at first raged at my budding radicalism, my interest in civil rights when I was in college. She told me she would kill herself if I ever got involved with a Black man. I did, at one point, and she didn't. She told me that lesbianism was unnatural, but when I insisted on being a lesbian, she said what she always said when we had a serious conversation, "You're the best daughter in the world," and I said, as I always did and meant it, "You're the best mother in the world." I still believe it — that she was the best possible mother in a white supremacist, capitalist heteropatriarchy.

I would trade years of my life to see her now as she was before the Alzheimer's disease, to learn the things she would never say — just what my father did to make her so unhappy.

We are both eternally children, crying alone in the night, no more mommy for me or daughter for her.

COME SUNDAY

Antonia Baquet

My mother, Regina Baquet, died in 1935. She had lived only forty-four years. They were hard-work, heartbreak years, with illnesses and deaths lacing the months and years together like ribbons. A proud and indomitable woman, she spent her life's energy rebelling against her natural inheritances of poverty, ignorance and inequality. In the days of shufflin' dances and mammy lullabyes, Mama sang a different song.

Mama was a pretty Creole woman, about five feet four inches tall with a good figure, on the plump side. Her skin was a high-yellow, and her green-gray eyes fringed with heavy black lashes flamed or darkened with her mood. Waves of black hair curled into bangs on her forehead.

Mama bounded from one task to another with enormous energy. Her moods were unpredictable: one hour she was laughing and singing, the next morose and melancholy. Sometimes she was pious and called on the Lord: "Dear Lord, help me to bear with this old white woman's stingy ways." Other times, she would cuss and send the object of her wrath to hell: "Well, dammit, she can go straight to hell and take all her damn food with her." When provoked, her temper sent everyone — mistress, servant, child and adult — scurrying.

Perhaps at age forty-four, Mama already felt the weight of the aged in her heart. At times, a weariness pervaded her entire being. Her hands were puffy, florid and work-worn. When she was not feeling well, her face became ashen. Varicose veins often stood out in red and blue welts on her legs at the end of a ten- or twelve- hour work day, and her eyes sunk into deep brown frames. But when she was feeling well, she glowed with a youthful vitality.

Come Day, Go Day, Sunday will come Some Day.

Many times I heard Mama moan that old Negro lament of despair and hope. But the Sunday she hoped for never came for Mama. She died as she had lived — working. In the twenties and early thirties, Mama, divorced from my father and with two young daughters to raise, worked as a live-in cook and housekeeper for the wealthy "Rice King of the South" Kaplan family of Crowley, Louisiana. When we arrived, our basement rooms were dreary, dirty, with cobwebs and soot, but we scrubbed and polished them to a shine in a short while.

During these years, Mama had high blood pressure. She suffered from headaches, dizziness and nausea. Periodically, her doctor would put her on a no-salt, bland diet and order her to bed for a few weeks. Usually, she remained in bed for a few days; then, concerned about the disorganized melee of the household and the inconvenience her illness caused the Kaplans, and fearful of losing her job, Mama resumed her normal duties.

After my sister moved to Detroit, Mama sent me to visit her every summer for vacation. Usually I was home by mid-August for school opening, but when fall came the year Mama died, I still had not returned home, nor had I made plans to enter Southern University at Baton Rouge as Mama wished. I'd come home to spend Thanksgiving and Christmas with my mother, and to talk about plans for my future. As grownup as I thought I was, I'd been lonesome for Mama and homesick for Crowley. It felt good to be home.

The morning of December 12, 1935, dawned foggy and gray. Clouds hung heavy and low, and at seven o'clock, when Mama came into my room, no light filtered through the windows. She opened the curtains and greeted me cheerfully.

"Mornin', *chere*. Look here what your Mama brought you, *le petite dejeuner*, just what you like."

She placed a silver tray on the bed. There was strong drip coffee, thick country cream, plump hot biscuits and homemade fig preserves. Mama smiled and teased me: "Only the rich get this kind of service, *chere*, but this is your *laniappe* for all the work you did yesterday."

Growing up, I had dreamed of having breakfast in bed served on a silver tray. It had always typified the zenith of wealth and luxury. Mama knew of my fantasy, and sometimes, when I was a good helper or brought home an excellent report card, she would serve me breakfast in bed and call it my *laniappe*, my special treat.

[177]

Mama stayed and chatted for a few minutes and then left the room. I lingered over the last drop of coffee, then dressed and went up to the kitchen, where she was beginning preparation for the Southern noon dinner. I entered the kitchen with the tray in my hand, feeling good about being with Mama and being babied again.

"Mama, that really was a good treat," I told her as I kissed her cheek. "I don't know why, but nobody in Detroit makes biscuits like you do. Fact is, Ma, those northern folk just don't know how to cook."

Obviously pleased, Mama smiled and nodded in agreement. She had been to Detroit once and had come to the same conclusion. We finished cleaning up the breakfast dishes and she began cutting up ingredients for a seafood gumbo. As we worked, we talked small talk until she paused, glanced at me, and in a changed tone said, "You know, *chére*, I am worried about you stayin' up North without goin' to college. You know how your sister Eleanora studied hard to prepare herself to make a livin' before she left home. Eleanora had real good sense about that." She looked at me, then hurried on. "I just wish you'd come back home and go to Southern, or even Xavier. You could stay with your Aunt Antonia like Eleanora did."

I knew the subject would come up sooner or later. But I also knew it wasn't as easy as Mama made it out to be. Eleanora had taught school and contributed to her college education. How could I help pay? Four years seemed like an eternity to me, an eternity that included continued drudgery for Mama, who had already worked and sacrificed away her life for us. She looked at me earnestly, waiting for an answer.

"Mama, I think I should get out on my own now. The sisters at Saint Theresa's gave me a good high school education," I said with a bravado I didn't feel. "And anyway, where would the money for college come from?"

"Oh, but *chére*," she said excitedly, "Mr. Kaplan said he would sign a note for me to get the money we need from his bank for your first year. And I saved up a little too. After that, we can work something out with him."

Bewildered, incredibly naive for my years, I didn't know what to do. I had left Mama for five months and was thinking, guiltily, of leaving her again to do what I wanted to do, not what she wanted me to do. I had become enamored with the city and anxious to be independent like my sister.

"Mama, what do you think about me studying something that doesn't take as long to complete and isn't as expensive?" I grasped at something I knew a little about. "Something like beauty culture? That's a good business up North and you know how I like to play around with make-up and all that stuff." I plunged in, improvising as I went along. "There's a beauty school a few blocks from Eleanora's apartment. I could walk there every morning and save bus fare. Maybe I should find out more about it."

"*Oui*, that's all right with me," she said resignedly. "*S'il vous plait*. It sure is better than nothin'. Maybe you could go to school in Detroit, then come back here and open your own shop. A beauty shop is good for business down here, too."

Abruptly, as if weary of the troublesome conversation, she changed the subjects. "*Chére*, that breakfast room floor is filthy. I think I'll give it a good scrubbin' this mornin'."

She got a bucket of soapy water and some rags, rolled down her stockings and walked into the breakfast room. Suddenly, I heard a small moan. I dropped the kitchen towel and rushed into the room. She was on her knees, holding her head.

"Mama, Mama, what's the matter?" I cried.

Still holding her head, she muttered, "My head hurts."

I began to lift her as I screamed to the Kaplan's chauffeur, "Mr. Leslie, Mr. Leslie, come quick. Mama's real sick. Oh, Mr. Leslie, hurry!"

He came running, and together we carried Mama to my bedroom. I saw her look back at the overturned bucket, the puddle of water and her unfinished job. But she was silent as we laid her on the bed.

We called the white doctor in Crowley who had been treating Mama. He came right away and gave her an injection. I saw him shake his head as he talked to Mr. Leslie. My heart pounded, and I was afraid to ask Mr. Leslie what the doctor had said. Someone called our parish priest. In minutes he arrived, and I heard him intone: "Out of the depth I cry to Thee." Although I had never witnessed it, I knew he was giving her the Rites of Extreme Unction, the Last Rites: "Oh, Lord, hear my prayer."

Around noon, Mama slipped into a coma. All I could do was sit by the bed and watch her. As I held her limp hand, she began to utter strange sounds. Someone led me outside. I stumbled out of the darkened room, into the big basement that I had so long ago cleaned, decorated and made believe was a palace.

I rocked back and forth and cried and prayed. "Good Lord, don't let her die working, please don't let her die working."

Then someone came, held me firmly and said softly, "*Chére*, your Mama gone now." I murmured, "What time is it?" "Three o'clock," someone answered. Same time Jesus died on the cross, I thought.

I began to cry and scream, "Where can I take Mama now? Lord, I didn't want her to die in this basement."

In those times, the deceased were prepared for burial by the mortician, then brought home and placed in front parlors. Relatives and friends kept constant vigil until the day of the funeral, usually three or four days later.

Miss Cora, Mama's best friend, who had been there all along, took charge. "*Chére*, you come right now to my house and stay. I'll tell them to bring your Mama there." She put her arms around me. "We'll have the wake there."

Mr. Leslie went back upstairs to call my sister in Detroit. Then I remembered that Miss Julie, the young mistress of the house, was in Houston visiting her sister. I asked Mr. Leslie to call and tell her to come home at once.

"I already called Miss Julie," Mr. Leslie answered in a flat tone. He looked away as he said it.

"When will she be back?" I asked.

He turned towards me. "She said she can't come home now." His voice was so low I could hardly hear him. "She said there's nothing she could do if she came back." I stared at him in disbelief. Nothing she could do? Whatever Miss Julie's troubles, there was always something Mama could do. Mama had never let Miss Julie down. She'd stayed up all night, every night, when Maurice, Miss Julie's baby, was fretful, acted as her personal maid, planned menus, managed servants and was always her confidante in troubled times. Now Miss Julie said there's nothing she can do. Into my scrambled emotions, a troublesome thought emerged: Mama can't serve her anymore. Mama isn't useful to her anymore. I guess we never mattered to her—just two good colored servants. She's just like all the rest. Murderer, I thought. You worked Mama to death. I hate you!

I turned my back on my white and gold ruffled room, a silent witness to our lives, and the collapse of the world we knew. I stumbled out of the polished basement, past Mama's dark and silent room, past her old sewing machine, past the bouquet of dried fall leaves I had arranged yesterday near the entrance.

Outside, the rain fell. Mr. Leslie got the limousine out of the garage and drove Miss Cora and me across town to her home. Just as he had driven Mama and me to the Kaplan house that first day, when I held tightly onto Mama's hand; that day long ago, when I was a child and the sun was shining and I was safe and secure.

The news of Mama's sudden death preceded us and raced through all sections of Crowley, black and white. When we arrived at Miss Cora's house, people were already gathered.

I went into a bedroom and wept.

I didn't want to see Mama in the casket with candles at each end. Everyone told me I'd feel better when I saw how pretty and peaceful she looked. I didn't want her to look peaceful. Mama never looked peaceful. Happy, sad, angry, petulant. But never peaceful.

Finally, I walked to the casket and looked at Mama. She lay, with her curly black hair over her forehead and her poor, work-worn hands clasped together, holding her worn-out brown rosary. I wanted to raise her arms and circle them above her head, the way she did when she found a minute to rest. Nothing was better.

Memories overwhelmed me. I remembered the time we were on the train to New Orleans. Mama wore her old black coat with the frizzy fake fur collar. I sat across the aisle, ashamed of her. I thought of the time I shut the door in her face; the fancy clothes I wore; the trips I took. These things weighed on me as I looked at Mama, in a gray casket with pink satin lining. People came and went. Many wept silently, others audibly.

A thick blanket of glorious red roses lay across the casket;

a white ribbon with gold letters announced simply: *Kaplan Family.*

I wanted to tear the roses off and trample them. The priest and nuns recited the rosary. Candles burned softly. The aroma of brewing coffee mingled with the sickening sweet fragrance of flowers. Miss Cora gave me warm soup and Eleanora begged me to stop crying. But I could no more stop crying than I could make Mama hear me murmuring over and over again, "Mama, I am sorry."

Then I knew that Mama was dead. Mama was gone from me forever. Mama would never sing, cuss, cry, pray, work or give again.

Sunday had come, after all.

MY RIGHT ARM

Betty Taylor-Thompson

I was reared by a community of three beautiful, strong, Black women. I lived with my mother and my grandmother, and I was nurtured, educated, and spent most of my elementary days close to my aunt in the schools where she was a teacher and later a principal. All these women left their marks squarely on my personality, values, heart and soul. I have now physically lost each one, my aunt to high blood pressure, stroke and heart disease, then my grandmother to the same things plus an operation I have never understood. Then my mother broke her hip in the back yard feeding the dogs and fell into a coma during an operation to fix the hip. Mother never awoke; she was seventy-one.

It is very difficult to live without your right arm, especially if you are right-handed. Everything you do depends on your right arm and its extension, your hands and fingers. When it is gone it is virtually impossible to function as a whole human being, and that is how I have felt — not like a whole person, since Mama's been gone from this earth.

I have listened to all the clichés — "It was her time"— "If you weren't strong enough, God would not have taken her"— "Just pray and everything will be all right!!!" — and various other well-intentioned phrases. But when it comes right down to it, I can't ask questions or get any information or advice from the one and only person I could always trust to be on my side. It is a great loss. It is the loss of my right arm.

I was her only child. I did not have to share that relationship with anyone else. No matter what happened, she was all mine. There is something special about being an "only." I was in college before I fully appreciated that fact.

I did not have a conventional mother or a conventional family. I lived with mother and grandmother and cousins and occasionally an assortment of children my mother brought home from her classroom for various humanitarian reasons. I was happy. My mother did not cook, nor did she clean. My mother did not comb hair, but did a mean pincurl when I turned twelve and grew out of plaits. My mother went to work every-day as a teacher and then as a principal. She was a career woman in the forties, fifties, sixties, seventies. She even made it into the eighties. She was a modern, liberated woman before it was fashionable.

I now realize that she had none of the "hangups" that many of her contemporaries had. She was a chemistry major and math minor at a time when women did not major in such subjects, especially Black women. She played a vigorous game of tennis and had lots of boyfriends. She planned and executed the Freshman Revenge against the upperclassmen, flooding the freshman dormitory and causing damage that her beloved father and patient mother paid for. When I went to the same college where some of the same people who knew her were still around, they expected something exciting from her child. I turned out to be a disappointing pansy. I did not live up to her reputation. I went through college as a pale ghost of my mother's reputation — a quiet, shy, retiring wallflower and wet blanket.

Many of my friends' mothers are still living, and every time I see them I feel jealous and cheated. Why did I lose my mother is a question I will always ask. I would have welcomed the privilege of being able to do something for my aging mother. But she was taking care of me to the last, and when she couldn't take care of herself, she was in a coma. I felt cheated. I begged her to live. I prayed for her to live. I offered myself in her place and even offered my children. I begged and pleaded and finally after almost a month of no response, I asked God either to give her back or take her, for I knew that my mother would hate the vegetative state.

I was with her when she died. I knew she was taking her last breaths. I heard the so-called "death-rattle" in her throat through the breathing tube. I held her hand and kissed her and loved her past the end.

I went to her funeral, which was rushed because the minister said he had to go out of town, and wanted to do the ceremony himself. I was vaguely dissatisfied with the ceremony. When the minister said Mother had died alone, I was horrified. *She had waited for me*, I wanted to scream. But like a good little girl, I sat there, quietly weeping. There were numerous people at my mother's funeral. She had been well loved, a teacher and principal for over forty years. Her students, colleagues, friends and admirers were there. En route to the cemetery, the procession of cars was so long I could not see the end.

Other people's reaction to my mother's death continues to amaze me after seven years. People left their jobs and couldn't bear to see me because they said I looked too much like her. I was resentful, hurt. People she had befriended were no longer friends to me. Even my relatives treated me differently. It was as I suspected. Nobody liked me; they only liked her. When she was no longer around, they had no use for me. I went inside myself and stayed for years, never trusting anyone or anything. If my mother could be taken from me then nothing I had was safe.

Everything that happened to me after her death showed I wasn't safe. My health dissipated. My half-sister remarked that I had gone through every disease from A to P before I finally got pneumonia a little less than a year after her death. I had needed an operation before she died. I finally got it six months after her death, and I almost died. The whole thing went wrong. I got a postoperative infection that only one out of a thousand people ever get, and I sustained a hideous scar from all the clamps and stitches breaking. Every time I look at the scar I know it is the physical scar of her death. The other scars in my heart and in my mind are deeper and not visible to the eye; they are much worse.

Since my mother's death, I have tried to fill her space in my life with other things. I started aerobics, joined a new health club and exercised fiercely when I wasn't sick. Now I have a job that consumes much of my extra time. Like Mother, I have learned to lose myself in work. I am amazed at how I am like her physically and mentally. I now see things about my mother that I could have never understood had she been alive. Often I lie awake at night and try to figure out if something she said or did can guide me in the understanding of myself. She often said, "I don't know enough to tell you what to do. I haven't been that successful in human relations myself." What she really meant was that she had not been successful with marriage and men, and neither have I. I now have a seemingly great relationship and marriage, but even that is directly related to her influence because she introduced me to my present husband.

Since she died, I each morning wake up and wonder how I am going to get through another day. When she was alive, I never wondered how I would complete the day or why I would complete it. I did well in college for her; I went to graduate school because I wanted her to be proud of me and know I did not waste her hard-earned dollars; I got my Ph.D. for her; I cared for my children for her; I went to church for her. Now that she is gone, I realize that when one does everything because of and for someone else, either one thinks very little of herself or a great deal of that someone else. It has been a painful realization.

People thought that I would not mentally survive her death. Somehow she managed to give me enough strength to live, and I still draw on her spirit each day in order to continue. I know Mother would love me even when I don't love myself. Her tolerance and generosity were almost unlimited. She made few judgments; she said little and did not offer explanations for the limitations of others. She never gossiped.

I depended on Mother to give me that golden glow of life. I lived through her exploits and her excitements. I long for her each morning when I wake and each night when I go to sleep. I see her in my mirror urging me on. I no longer have to pull over to the side of the road in my car, cry and try to rid myself of the stabbing pain. The pain has now dulled and partially healed. But like arthritis on a rainy day, it returns to remind me that the limb is missing.

XMAS '89

Maureen Sangster

It's approaching Xmas and I feel my mother getting closer. Already I'm thinking— what can I give her as a present? But she's dead. She died at the end of May. My brother and I had not been expecting her death.

There'll be no phone call now in which she asks me what my plans are for Xmas. No chance for me to become irritated by that question. No chance for me to repeat, to my partner and friends, my cliched complaints about family duty and the awfulness of my mother. No phone call.

One shop in the village where I live has already hung its Xmas decorations — looped golden streamers round its walls and placed a Merry Xmas sign, of red letters, in its bow-window. Fake snow rests in the corners of the small upper window-panes. The effect is joyful and welcoming. Xmas is coming.

Once upon a time my mother cooked Xmas dinner for nine people. We ate it, seated in the living-room. A full four course meal, too much food really and eaten too early in the day. Gradually over the years, the people round that table died: a granny, a granpa, the other granny, the cousin, a friend, my father. In the end, with my brother kept busy, I spent Xmases alone with my mother.

These occasions were grim. We'd eat the obligatory bird. My mother would remember something awful I'd said to her when I was ten. Dead dad's hat was still on the hatstand in the hall. Though she had strung up Xmas cards above the mantel-piece, she had stopped, as she said, "bothering about a tree." She was alone in Aberdeen, had witnessed too many deaths, been attendant on too many of the dying. What use was a Xmas tree, its lights glowing in a dark, unused front room?

I fell in love and moved in with Kenny. I no longer returned home every Xmas. She managed. She was strong.

After a twenty-five year absence from the classroom, she'd gone back to teaching after my father died. She'd also learnt to drive, though, typically she'd say, when picking me up at the station, "If only you could drive me." She always meant me to feel guilty.

Once I'd broken the annual ritual of going back north at Xmas, it became easy for me to forget her sadness. I nurtured contempt for her neediness. I hated the way she still looked to her children to give hope for the future. As her life contracted through illnesses, early retirement and the selling of her car, I ignored how lonely she was. And now I can't remember when I last spent Xmas with my mum.

Her last Xmas was a happy one, though. My brother and his wife spent it with her. I can imagine my mother airing beds, hanging bedcovers out on the line in preparation and telling both sets of neighbours, "My son and his wife are spending Xmas with me." She loved visitors.

She loved ceremonies. At Hallowe'en, we went round the house in the dark, turnip lantern in hand, swinging its stubborn light into every room, every cupboard to chase all evil spirits away. We even went out to the garden sheds. This year, I asked Kenny to do this with me. It seemed important. A lesson learnt about the imagination.

Like my mother, I now keep all the Xmas tree decorations together. I have them in a biscuit tin. She kept them in a worn cardboard box. In each case, that lovely feeling of opening up, year after year, a box that contains prettiness — silvery tinsel, gold tinsel, small bells, a little fat santa, a yellow bird with an open beak, twin angels, wooden shapes and sparkling balls. Most of these decorations come from her house, now sold. My favourite is a pink bell with a cat's face as its handle. I remember it hanging on the Xmas tree back home.

I want to create the magic of ceremonies because that is what my mother did, finding in Xmas, Hallowe'en, Bonfire Night and New Year a gift of security, a potent gesture-filled time with symbolism guaranteed. At these times, anxieties were soothed.

If I buy a real tree, well-proportioned and beautiful and place it in our window and pray for snow and hang Xmas cards up and put coloured lights and decorations onto the tree and then attend a candlelit watchnight service, maybe my mother will visit me. Her dignified spirit will walk up to me, her hands held out. I shall hold her as I never did, murmuring "Ruth . . . mum" against her surprisingly soft cheek.

She died at the edge of a wood, in a hospital called Woodend. There I discovered she was a woman called Ruth as well as my mother. There she stopped being the monster I had fleshed out over the years.

On every visit, I walked through the tall leafy trees up to the hospital. I felt their tall strength. The way they reached for the sky may have entered into her and, if she visits me, soon I'll want her to enter me, too. I shall be the tree my mother grew.

AN UNFINISHED STORY

Bookda Gheisar

I have imagined walking up to my mother's grave hundreds of times. I have imagined reading her name on the headstone. But it seems very unreal to imagine her lying underneath the earth. Perhaps I would feel differently if someday soon I visited her grave in Iran.

My mother, Azar, was a very beautiful woman. Her unusually light skin and blue eyes drew much attention to her, so when it came time for her to marry, she had many choices. She had been in love with a man of whom her family did not approve and, filled with anger, sadness and disappointment, decided to marry my father, whom she did not love. She was nineteen years old, he was thirty, and from the onset of their marriage he was unavailable, distant and involved in other relationships. I recall many winter evenings when my sister and I sat with our mother around the stove waiting for our father to come home. During those years my mother's energy was completely invested in changing her marriage. Many of her feelings towards my father were placed on me, and she became more and more distant as a mother. I spent many years feeling that my "badness" had ruined her life and that if I could become "good," things would improve. I wanted so much to please my mother and to be more like her. I longed for a peaceful and loving mother-daughter connection, unlike ours with its anger and resentment.

When I was thirteen years old, my mother attempted suicide. She had been very unhappy, and on this particular day she asked my sister and me to be very quiet because she needed some time to herself in her room. From behind the closed door I could hear music and the unbearable sound of her weeping. I took my sister, Makda, out into the street to play with some other children. I pretended to be playing until my anxiety became intolerable, and I ran to the neighbor's house, asking them to come check on my mother. Walking into her room, I immediately saw the bottle of pills next to her and her limp hand hanging down from the bed. Her face looked pale, and she seemed to be in a deep sleep. She was rushed to the hospital by the neighbors. Although my mother survived this suicide attempt, I felt the reality of her inevitable death for the first time.

A few years later things started to get a lot better for her. She became more involved with her family and friends, and her best friend moved in with us. I remember one afternoon in the middle of summer lying next to her while she read a magazine. We were both getting sleepy with the sun shining in our faces and the air conditioner humming. She asked me to brush her hair, softly. I could not move. The pain of our distance was so overwhelming that even the thought of being close and touching was unbearable. It was almost as if brushing her hair would have reminded me of how much I longed for closeness, and I was unwilling to face those feelings. This is a contradiction that both my mother and I felt, and I live to this day wanting so much to be close and feel love for each other, and yet fearing so much the loss of our relationship that it is impossible to become close. Years later, when I returned to Iran for a visit, I woke up from a nap and found my mother brushing my hair. We both cried, grieving the loss of the relationship we never had.

When I was fifteen years old, I was sent to school in the U.S. My family feels that I wanted to leave, that I pushed my mother until she agreed. I feel my mother sent me away because she felt their lives would be easier without me. We all felt rejected for many years, each blaming the other for the separation. I managed to visit my family in Iran a few times, the last time six years ago. At that time my mother told me that she planned to come to the U.S. for an extended visit. She said she longed to be away from my father and was ready to begin a life of her own. I began to dream of having her at my house, taking care of her and finding some way of being close to her at last. Three years ago, my mother made her final plans for leaving Iran. A few days before she was to leave Iran, she died of a sudden heart attack at the age of forty-seven. I never had a chance to see her again or say goodbye.

My family didn't tell me about her death until six months later. It is still unclear why I was not told until then, and in many ways this has contributed to my feeling the outsider in the family. The combination of living in a country thousands of miles away from my family, not being able to participate in a family ritual to say goodbye to my mother, and not being able to speak Farsi with my friends here in the U.S. made it seem impossible for me to understand how to grieve and let go of her in my life. My deepest and most painful feelings came in Farsi and because I was unable to share them with anyone, I was left feeling very distant from myself.

For almost a year after I learned of my mother's death my dreams focused on how I could have prevented her death. I would write and rewrite the story of her life in my dreams. And when she was ill I would always be there with her and I would be able to make her pain go away. In my waking life I have dreamed of living her dreams for her. I feel responsible and loyal to the life that she left unfinished, feeling that perhaps there is some way I can bring a happy ending to it. Sometimes I feel loyalty means having the things she always wanted and never had. But when I am happy, I feel I am being disloyal by having more than she had.

It was been difficult to figure out what it means to be loyal and how to remember the life of a person so close to you who is no longer there. After I found out about her death I had no idea how I would continue to remember her. I was scared of forgetting the sound of her voice, the color of her eyes, the way she smiled. I had to keep concrete reminders of her around. I put her pictures around the house. I wore a sweater she had knitted for me, over and over again. I kept some of my mother's clothes in the closet where I could see them everyday.

My mother is still often in my dreams. In one dream, I had just found out about her death, and I was devastated. I wanted to reread the letters she had sent. I was obsessed with remembering the last thing she had told me. I searched the whole house for her letters and finally remembered that I had thrown them all away. I sobbed and sobbed, finally becoming angry with myself. A friend of mine entered the room and asked, "Are you looking for the box of letters?" I said, "Yes, but I threw them away. They're not here." She pointed to the corner of the room and said, "They are right there." I looked and realized they had been there all along, right next to me.

LOOKING FOR MY MOTHER

Helen Vozenilek

"What have you done with the last ten years of your life?" my mother demands. My back stiffens like an animal sensing attack. It is the end of August and I have finally gathered enough courage to call home.

I never simply picked up the phone and called my mother. Anxiety would surge through my stomach as I'd rehearse possible conversations and outcomes. We did not call each other to share recipes or neighborhood gossip as I have imagined some mothers and daughters do — the close friend/confidante sort of relationship I thought I would give anything to have.

I have spent much of the past summer exploring the deep gnashing hole of hunger in myself. I think my sorrow and tears are for my biological mother leaving me when I was born. I do not know they are also in preparation for the leaving of the mother who raised me. I am not prepared for another parting.

"I just called to see how you were," I begin cautiously after I reach my mother on the second try.

"Not very well," she answers. She sounds tired, slightly out of breath. The last time we'd spoken was on Mother's Day; she had already been through two chemotherapy cycles. She'd made a comment about how disgusting Rock Hudson was and I got off the phone shortly afterwards. In the past few months, I'd been unable to get much information from my brother. His laconic replies over the phone assured me that she was fine and getting better.

"I called you earlier but no one was home." I feel inadequate and on guard. I'm never really sure what to say to my mother, and even less so now that she's ill. She is both a medical doctor and my mother. I've never seen her in anything but control.

"I'm surprised to hear from you in the middle of the day,"

she launches in. "You're out of work again? On unemployment? "

"I had surgery on my hand a few weeks ago," I offer in my defense. "The carpal tunnel stuff."

"You shouldn't be doing work like that. It's men's work. I don't know what it is you are trying to prove."

Three years earlier, when our relationship was the closest it had ever been, she had been sympathetic about my hand. She'd even called me with information about a special ratchet-type screwdriver. Now she is clearer about the responsibility for the problem. The tentative steps we had been taking to traverse the huge gulf between us had stopped. Suddenly. And reversed. During the last nine months of her life, our relationship disintegrated as quickly and completely as did her health.

"Everything you do is against me, is to spite me. The work you do, the people you know, the causes you believe in." My mother is on her favorite litany. I imagine a ledger in front of her on which my trespasses are detailed. The list is long. The accusations are not new, only tidier, chronological. She fires them at me. The conversation is not yet three minutes old and already I am skidding and stuttering in my defense.

"That's not true," I say repeatedly. "You are being ridiculous." At other times, I snap back, "Yeah, sure, right." I am trying not to creep under the familiar and comforting blankets of silence, sullenness and sarcasm.

"Even when you were little you snuck around, did things behind my back," she continues her review. "Criticized me, found fault with everything I did."

It was true. All of my friends had perfect mothers. Mine was too strict, too European. At ten, I wanted to move in with my friend Diane because her mother was nice and did anything Diane wanted. I told my mother that. At age fifteen, I did move out of my mother's house. Later, a therapist asked me to imagine how my mother must have felt when I said I didn't want to live with her. I didn't think of it at the time. I was fifteen. I thought only of myself.

My mother is surveying the landscape of the past twenty-eight years with me. Only later do I understand the reasons for her review. I jump in correcting, challenging her version. I remind myself to be strong — keep the quiver out of my voice, check the tears filling my eyes. I can count on one hand the number of times I've seen my mother cry. I'm always the one who breaks down. On the uneven abacus of our relationship, it is another area where she is in control.

We talk for nearly half an hour. For us, it is a long time. Towards the end, when it seems we've replayed decade-old tapes and exhausted all new dialogue, I say, "Well, I don't know that we are getting anywhere. I guess I just wanted to call and let you know that I'm thinking of you and I care for you very much."

"Helen, I care for you very much, too, and wish you well." my mother answers.

Do I detect a catch in her voice or is it mine echoing through the receiver?

Two weeks later I am grateful we have at least been able to say this much. The phone call reaches me at work. "Your mother is dead."

At my mother's house, my brother and his wife are in complete control. Lists are drawn up, friends and acquaintances called, service and burial arrangements made. I walk around in a daze, an extra on a newly released script.

I am desperate to understand the last months, weeks, days, hours of my mother's life. In the house I find two wigs, a walker, an eggcrate mattress, a medicine cupboard filled with pills. In the medical reports, I read of missed appointments, hospitalizations, fevers, weakness, weight loss and the persistent hope by her doctors that chemotherapy would work, remission would come. And the terse entry three days before she died, beginning, "Myra is not doing terribly well."

"What did my mother say? How did she act? Was she in pain?" I ask my mother's best friend. "Did she know she was dying?"

"Your mother was a very private person," Judy answers. "No one really knew her."

I feel sad and slightly vindicated. Sad that my mother kept things to herself and was alone at the end. Vindicated to learn that it wasn't just me who couldn't get in.

Almost immediately I set to rummaging through my mother's belongings. Sifting through papers, files, drawers, cabinets, I'm only vaguely aware of what I'm looking for. A notebook, perhaps a journal, some written clue to my mother's identity. But writing is my mode of communication, not my mother's. My writing made her nervous, presenting a world I didn't share with her, a world she couldn't see into. She and my brother would scream at each other across the kitchen, while I stood by silently, wishing for the noise to stop. Their disagreements would erupt and then disperse as easily as a steam blast on a winter's day. Ours would fester, never quite surface and never quite clear.

Desperately I search for some letter left unsent to me, one in which our difficulties are neatly framed and explained. The one where she ends by telling me how much she loves me. The one she never sent me. The one I never sent her.

Her medical certificates fill one wall of the study. I find her immigration papers, her citizenship papers, pictures from her life and family on another side of the world. She has saved my brother's and my report cards, class photos, newspaper articles, awards. Travel books, brochures, language tapes, postcards testify to her rediscovered passion for travel. In a manila envelope, I find the cards and letters from me she has kept. I take these with me to read later. I am embarrassed by their emptiness, so little do they say and share.

I never shared much with my mother. I didn't tell her about the plays I was in at school, the field trips we went on, the awards I'd won. The older I got, the more I concealed. I wouldn't tell her about my friends, my political beliefs and actions, my concerns and what really was important to me. I lied not so much with words, but with their absence — with silence. "Why, why?" she would hammer at me after she'd found out something I'd withheld. "Why must you keep secrets?" I couldn't tell her. I didn't know why. I still don't know why. All I could see were the lines from a paperback I'd seen somewhere that read: "Why don't I tell you who I am? Because if I do and you don't like it, that is all I have."

Exactly one year after my mother's death, I am on a plane to Prague. I think that this trip to my mother's origins will help snap the cold steel of despair and lassitude that has girded me these past twelve months.

[196]

With my mother's brother George I walk through the section of Prague where my mother was raised. I stare fixedly at buildings, take photos, jot notes in my journal. I anticipate some jolt of discovery, some bolt of understanding, when I retrace the steps of her past. But my imagination is paltry. The city, with its centuries-old bridges, castles and churches, its cobbled, narrow and winding streets makes me think more of Kafka than of my mother.

I meet another of my mother's brothers. He does not look at me once; there was bad blood between my mother and him. I cannot take my eyes off of him . He looks almost exactly like my mother: the same high, broad forehead, brown eyes, thin brow, full nose. As an adopted child, I have not grown up thinking that individuals in families look alike. I am fixated. I am curious about my mother's relationship with her parents and brothers. Her whole family was thrown into prison in retaliation after she escaped from Czechoslovakia in 1948. This I learn from other people, not my mother. I want to know more.

"Why does Camel not like me?" I ask George that evening.

"No, no, you he like. Much problems with Myra," he answers either unwilling or unable to say more. Another uncle does not even make an effort to see me.

Driving through the green rolling hills and villages of southern Bohemia and picking mushrooms in the forests around Prague, I feel my mother most strongly. I am happy and want to believe this is her happiness I am sharing.

"My mother, she likes pick *houby*?" I ask George, holding up a mushroom. "She like come here in woods?"

"Yoh, Myra like cook with *houby*."

The language barrier between us is huge and distressing. I do not even try to frame the more complex questions. I feel I'm at the center of something critical, but don't know how to focus the lens. I spend days gazing distractedly into the Vltava River. Sometimes a weariness as heavy as the stone bridge spanning the banks hangs in my soul. Other times I am as numb as the morning fog that glances on the water's edge. When my train pulls from the Prague station three weeks later, I am more than ready to leave.

My mother is not alive to witness the Velvet Revolution in

Czechoslovakia in November 1989. I wonder if she would have gone home to visit and if I would have shared her bittersweet joy. Last year I learned of George's death. I was crushed, for he was a wonderful human being. Also, I have imagined him as the last link to my mother. That, too, now severed.

I don't see my mother in my dreams anymore. I no longer hear her across the store shouting my name, or spot her at a nearby restaurant table. I don't rush to the mailbox hoping to find a letter from her, or expect to hear her voice over the answering machine. I finger her hand-knit sweaters and colorful silk scarves tucked neatly away in my bottom clothes drawer. Her smell lingers only faintly.

Her presence takes other forms. Her absence fills other senses.

I've taken to reading stories, analyses, descriptions of the mother-daughter relationship. I look for stories similar to my own, for theories to explain our interactions, reasons why my mother was the way she was and why I am like I am. Usually it all works very well in my head. But when I feel lonely and motherless, words become impoverished bedfellows that irritate in their clumsiness.

I look back through my notebooks and journals of the past five years. I find scores of pieces written to my mother, for my mother, about my mother. Some are a few sentences long, others go on for a couple of pages. None are finished. This is the first story I've completed. And how unfinished it feels.

I think about Dorothy's search for Oz, her encounters with different people, her travels to far-off lands and her final discovery that all along she had the power to return to Kansas, her family and herself. A large part of me is waiting for the Good Witch to tell me what to do. A large part of me wants to believe that a simple wave of a magic wand will direct me home. But I suspect that, like Dorothy, certain travels and labors must take place. And I'll have to look for awhile before I can click my heels together and go home.

• • • •

——————— BIOGRAPHIES ———————

Mothers and Daughters

DAISY ALDAN has been called "a major poet" by *World Literature Today*. Her recent book, *In Passage* was nominated for a Pulitzer. Her novella, *A Golden Story*, was published with a grant from the National Endowment for the Arts. Its sequel, *Day of the Wounded Eagle*, has recently been published by the LeMay Company, New York. In 1989, she received the ALTA Literary Translation Award from the University of Texas and in 1990, the AGATE Educator Recognition Award.

ESTHER EDELHEIT FINFER was the mother of Daisy Aldan. As a girl of fifteen, she arrived in New York City from Austria. She was a major actress in the Yiddish Theatre in New York City, who with her brothers, organized the Yiddishe Volksbuhne (The Jewish Folk Theatre), still in existence. She also acted in silent films. At age sixty, she began exhibiting her paintings in major galleries, and at eighty, she received the Los Angeles City of Hope award for her recitations in their behalf. During the Depression, she led a hunger march to Washington, and during World War II, she was made a General for selling one million dollars' worth of war bonds.

JUDY A. ASHLEY recently completed her B.A. in psychology at the age of forty and began attending graduate school in the fall of 1991 working toward her M.S. in counseling. Her interests include death and dying issues including bereavement, feminism (it is not a dirty word), AIDS, holistic health and the unique qualities of each individual. She enjoys reading, writing, quiet times, good friends and the love of her husband, Walt McLaughlin.

DELVINA MARY RAYTA JEAN ASHLEY was a stubborn, independent, courageous woman who defied the trends at a time when women did not go outside traditional roles. Led by an inner strength that sometimes appeared as cold and abrasive, she felt deeply and died surrounded by love.

ANTONIA BAQUET, after retirement as a Department of Defense Systems Analyst, returned to school to study creative writing. "Come Sunday" is an excerpt from her book-in-progress, *Recollections of a Lil' Half-White, Stuck-Up Nigga*. She is the mother of the poet, Toi Derricotte.

REGINA BAQUET, often called "The Robin Hood of Crowley," worked day and night to help the poor and hungry. She was a Giver, an off-the-top, bottom-of-the-heart giver. A Louisiana Black woman, born in abject poverty, a generation removed from slavery, of stubborn strength, she refused to fit the Aunt Jemima image of her time.

JUDITH BARRINGTON is the author of *Trying to Be an Honest Woman* (1985) and *History and Geography* (1989), both published by The Eighth Mountain Press. She is co-founder of The Flight of the Mind, an annual summer writing workshop for women. Recently she wrote the libretto for an oratorio, *Mother of Us All* (music by David York), first performed March 1991 by Concord Choir.

VIOLET ELIZABETH HELENE BARRINGTON (born LAMBERT) grew up in Banstead, Surrey, England. After she married, she lived with her husband in Barcelona, Spain, where her first two children were born, until the outbreak of the Spanish Civil War, when she returned to England. She loved music, sunshine and laughter, and was a great gardener.

JOAN CAMPBELL's poems and essays have appeared in *The Ohio Review, Yankee, Southern Poetry Review* and *The American Voice*. Her story, "Why is the Moon Cracked?" won first prize in Crosscurrents' Annual Fiction Contest. She is currently working on completing a collection of poems and a book of essays about the creative process titled *The Ritual of Soul-Making*.

RUBY JACK PETERSON was the youngest of five children, born on an Iowa farm. She married and raised two children, was active in her church, and had a marvelous sense of humor, not to mention sense of adventure. Her daughter writes, "Once she gave me nearly a thousand dollars to teach me how to play roulette in Las Vegas. I got on a winning streak, with thousands of dollars soon stacked in front of me, until one turn of the wheel took it all away. She looked at me and laughed. 'That's roulette!' she said. Her freedom and nonconformity have helped me to live on the edge, with a constant sense of joy, and very little fear."

MARILYN ELAIN CARMEN has earned three college degrees. She has had her poetry published in such journals as *Heresies*, *Black American Literature Forum* and *Iris*. Her short stories have appeared in both the U.S. and England. She is the recipient of the 1990 Pennsylvania State Council of the Arts grant, based on an excerpt of *Blood on the Root*, a novella published in 1990 by Esoterica Press. She is currently at work on an autobiography entitled *A Walk Out of the Water*.

GENEVA R. FELTON SCRUGGS attended both Virginia Union University and Shippensburg State Teachers College. She received two scholarships. Upon graduating from William Penn High School in Harrisburg, Pennsylvania in 1936, she was recommended to Virginia Union without examination. Latin was the bane of her existence. She was quiet, intelligent, musical and creative.

ARUPA CHIARINI lives with her husband and stepson in Gainesville, Florida. She is a poet and playwright and was creative director of IDGAFFA (I Don't Give a Fart for Art), a women's theater troupe, momentarily defunct. She is also a core member of Acrosstown Repertory Theater, a community theater in Gainesville, which is dedicated to providing theater opportunities for working-class people, especially women and other minority groups.

EDITH FRANCES KING was a beautiful and intelligent woman. She survived the tragedies of an abusive childhood and a failure to bond with her first two children. She had an adventurous spirit. During the final years of her life she was a student of the teachings of George Gurdjieff.

SUSAN CHRISTIAN grew up in Austin, Texas, with her father, sister, stepmother and four half-brothers. She moved to Los Angeles in 1978 after graduating from the University of Texas. She works as a feature writer for the *Los Angeles Times*.

ELIZABETH ANNE BROWN was born and raised in the small West Texas town of Colorado City. She had five siblings, three of whom are still living. "Betty" Brown graduated from the University of Texas at Austin, where she met her husband, George

Christian, in journalism school. They were married in 1951. Betty died in 1957 at the age of twenty-nine. Her daughters remained close to her family in West Texas.

JOAN CONNOR's work has appeared many journals, among them: *The Worcester Review* , *Z Miscellaneous* , *Re: Artes Liberales* , *Athena* , and *Blueline*, in which "When Mountains Move" first appeared in slightly different form. She is currently working on her first novel begun on a fellowship at the Vermont Studio Colony.

MARY LYON CONNOR spent most of her adult life lame and in pain, as a result of a car accident during her first pregnancy, despite decades of failed attempts at corrective surgery. Writes her daughter, "Unhobbled in spirit, generosity and enthusiasm, she outran her entire family. We are still trying to catch up with her quick mind and brisk and easy laughter. She still leads the chase."

CAROL ANNE DOUGLAS is a lesbian feminist who works on the newspaper *off our backs*. Her published works include *Love and Politics: Radical and Lesbian Feminist Theories* and a novel, *To the Cleveland Station*.

JOAN FLANNERY DOUGLAS was born in Baltimore in 1908; she was the fourth of eight children in an Irish Catholic family. She supported herself in a variety of occupations, including real estate and editing, until she married at age thirty-six. She loved her one daughter, Carol Anne, all of her relatives, and her garden. She died in 1986.

ROSE MARY FANDEL's realization of many dreams was unlocked at her mother's passing. She moved to Madison, Wisconsin, four years ago and achieved recognition as a performance artist, performing her poetry. The move brought wonderful changes to her ability to practice women's spirituality and to her personal life. This past year has brought the start of a relationship with a wonderful woman.

ELIZABETH M. CARROLL DAILY fought for her rights and the rights of others. She was instrumental in holding white flight to a minimum when integration was begun in her parish. An Army nurse during World War II, she later provided medical care for her neighborhood. At her death she became the first woman to be buried with military honors by her American Legion Post.

JYL LYNN FELMAN is an award-winning writer whose work can be found in *Tikkun, Bridges, Sojourner, Sinister Wisdom* and *Genesis 2*. Her work has appeared in various anthologies, including *The Tribe of Dina, Word of Mouth, Speaking for Ourselves* and *Korone* vol. 6. Her first collection of short fiction, *Hot Chicken Wings,* will be published by Aunt Lute books in Fall 1992.

EDITH JEANNE MAYER FELMAN was a vibrant, funny woman who was beloved by her students, proud to be a Jew and ambivalent that she had a lesbian daughter.

PATRICIA FLINN lives in Warren Township, New Jersey, with her husband, Eugene, who is also a writer. A co-author of the *Literary Guide to the United States,* her stories have appeared in *The Wisconsin Review, Painted Bride Quarterly* and *The Worcester Review,* among others.

HELEN CRAMER PEAN adored animals. She enjoyed feeding squirrels in the park and wild birds from her window sill. Her real love, however, was dogs. One day she picked up a cane, put on a pair of dark glasses and posed as a blind woman so that she and O'Casey, her daughter's dog, could dine together in a local restaurant. Unfortunately, both she and O'Casey were quickly ejected from the premises when she removed her glasses to read the menu in full view of an astonished but wary waitress.

BOOKDA GHEISAR was born and raised for the first half of her life in Tehran, Iran. She now lives in Seattle, Washington, and is in practice as a feminist therapist.

AZAR OMIDVAR was a strong, courageous and intelligent woman who was loved by many people. She challenged many peoples' stereotypes about women and raised two strong daughters and one son.

KAREN ANNE KANDIK was born in Sioux City, Iowa, and attended college in Mt. Vernon, Iowa, and Minneapolis. She lives in Minneapolis and is employed as a social work supervisor. She's single and has a cat. This is the first piece she has written for publication.

ESTHER CORA FRUEND KANDIK was born in 1920 in Lakewood, Ohio; died in 1982 in Sioux City, Iowa. Her years were filled with creating: a satisfying marriage, two independent children, a child care center named for her, the ability to take care of herself as well as she took care of others, and many treasured memories for family and friends.

ROSLYN LUND is an award-winning writer who has had published a novel, *The Sharing* (Morrow) and short stories (cited in Pushcard Prize and Best American).

MOLLIE MESSINGER, says her daughter, "was more sensitive and less harsh" than she appears in the story, "and we cared about each other in our own way — perhaps too deeply."

JUDITH McCOMBS has two books of poetry, *Sisters and Other Selves* (Glass Bell Press, Detroit) and *Against Nature: Wilderness Poems* (Dustbooks) and two scholarly books (both with G.K.Hall) — *Critical Essays on Margaret Atwood*, and an annotated Atwood bibliography, co-authored with Carole L. Palmer, called *Margaret Atwood: A Reference Guide*. In 1971 McCombs founded *Moving Out*, the nation's oldest surviving feminist literary arts journal. Her poetry, which includes a narrative series called "The Mother Poems," appears in *Calyx, Devil's Millhopper, Nimrod* (as a Neruda winner), *Poet Lore, Poetry, Prism,* the anthology *Sisters of the Earth,* and elsewhere; her fiction appears in *Bridge, Kansas Quarterly, Nimrod* and *Sun Dog* (as a finalist for their World's Best Short Short Story contest.)

THELMA ALBERTA SUTTERLIN McCOMBS was born to parents who farmed and dealt in livestock. She earned her way from a small Kansas farm to New York City in the Depression, married a mathematician, raised three children while traveling in most of the states with U.S. Coast and Geodetic Survey parties, and saw that her daughters as well as her son went to college. Her daughter says, "I remember her as chin-up determined, a daydreamer eager to move on, and at the end courageous and loving."

MOLLY MARTIN is not quite as smart as her mother, but she tries to live up to her example. An activist and electrician who lives in San Francisco, she is editor of the anthology *Hard-Hatted Women: Stories of Struggle and Success in the Trades* (Seal Press, 1988), and she has edited *Tradeswomen* magazine for the past several years.

FLORENCE ELEANOR MARTIN was the daughter of Swedish and Norwegian immigrants. She learned to read at a very young age and was a voracious reader all her life. She was a feminist and anti-war activist, a lover of history, and a collector of old things. She also gets high marks as a mother from her four children.

CHRISTINE MORIARTY is a lawyer in a small Illinois town where she lives with her husband and two small daughters. Much of her energy in the last few years has been devoted to altering her life sentence for herself and her daughters.

ELEANOR JULIA MORIARTY raised eight children who, in turn, helped raise each other.

FAYE MOSKOWITZ, Director of the Creative Writing Program at George Washington University in Washington, D.C., is author of *A Leak in the Heart* (David Godine, 1985), *Whoever Finds This: I Love You* (David Godine, 1988) and *And the Bridge is Love* (Beacon Press, 1991).

SOPHIE EISENBERG STOLLMAN, the youngest of thirteen children, came to this country from Poland at seventeen. She married Aaron Stollman and together they had four children. The eldest, a little girl, died at five, and Sophie never stopped mourning for her. Sophie was a fiercely loving mother. Who knows what else she might have become were it not for her untimely death at forty.

LAURA MUNTER-ORABONA is a thirty-nine year old electrician. She is a mixed blood (Puerto Rican/Swedish). Her mother was her model for the strength, invincibility and passion of women of color. "I miss her still."

LAURA MARIA-RAMIREZ ORABONA MUNTER was born in San Juan in 1921. At age fifty-four she died, long before she was ready. She said that her only regret was that she had so much yet to do. Her daughter says, "I could write a page of her achievements, the legacy of hope, pride and strength which extends like a rainbow. But what I remember most in my heart were the beautiful gardens she grew, the blossoming magnolias, how her face lit when I said, 'Mom, I have a garden, too,' and how rich I am that she was my mother."

GRACE PALEY and her mother: biographies withheld.

HERMINE PINSON, a native Texan, is presently an assistant professor of English at Texas Southern Univeristy as well as a poet and fiction writer. She has published work in *Faces Anthology*, *The Cultural Arts Review*, *Houston Poetryfest Anthology*, *Blonde on Blonde*, and *Common Bonds: Stories by and about Modern Texas Women*.

ENID IVY DAVIS HARRIS, says her daughter, "was herself a song and taught me what I know of music, a way to bring order to my life while I ride the notes to the other side."

SUE ROCHMAN is the Education Coordinator for Ithaca Rape Crisis and a freelance writer whose work focuses on AIDS, health care and prison issues. Raised in Los Angeles, she now lives in Ithaca, New York, with her cat Eiko.

MARSHA MIRIAM SOKOL ROCHMAN, an only child, had looked forward to the time she would be "Mom;" she gave her three daughters the type of childhood she had always wanted, but wasn't able, to have. In 1975 she returned to college to pursue a degree in Child Psychology — a dream cut short due to malignant melanoma, a form of skin cancer.

MAUREEN SANGSTER was born in 1954 in Aberdeen, NE Scotland. She now lives in Kirkcaldy, Fife, where she teaches creative writing to adults. Her poetry has been published in a variety of magazines and anthologies. She is now trying her hand at short stories.

RUTH MARGARET TAWSE loved the land and was a keen and successful gardener. She sang in the church choir and played the piano. As a young woman she'd won a medal for her singing. Firm in her views, she liked nothing better than a good argument.

SAPPHIRE is a poet, novelist and performance artist. She has self-published a book of poetry entitled *Meditations on the Rainbow*.

VIOLET DABNEY LOFTON was born August 1, 1920, the first of eight children, in Philadelphia. She left home at twenty-one to join the Army where she served for seven years. Her daughter says, "She told me once, 'You want something to write about? Well, I'll give you something to write about!' And she did."

JUDITH W. STEINBERGH is a writer and teacher in the Boston area. She has published four books of poetry; her most recent is *A Living Anytime*, prose poems (Talking Stone Press.) She is Writer-in-Residence in the Brookline Public Schools and performs and creates tapes for children and adults with Troubadour. "Traveling" and "Bathing" are in loving memory of:

ROSALYN LEVIN WOLINSKY "for her energy and bravery, a woman who loved people and community, who taught me to be welcoming and to reach out, who thought she'd be out playing golf to the very last day of her life," . . . Judith W. Steinbergh.

And:

CYNTHIA HARRIS SANVILLE "for her dignity and integrity. She taught her children, Doug, Barbara and me, that dying can be about living. This journey to the sea was her last gift, a memory affirming life," . . . Prilly Sanville.

BETTY TAYLOR-THOMPSON is a native of Houston, Texas, where she now lives and teaches English at Texas Southern University. She received her B.A. in English at Fisk University in Nashville, Tennessee, her M.L.S. in Library Science at Atlanta University, in Atlanta, Georgia, and her M.A. and Ph.D. in English from Howard Univeristy in Washington, D.C. Her primary interest and field of concentration is Afro-American literature and culture, and creative writing.

JOHNNIE HART TAYLOR BROOKS (1912 -1984), a native of Houston, Texas, worked for forty-seven years as a teacher and principal in the Houston Independent School District. She received a B.A. in chemistry at Fisk University in 1932. Because of financial and social restrictions, she became an elementary teacher and principal, and furthered her education by earning an M.S. degree in education at Texas Southern University and by doing further study at the University of Texas in reading education. Besides being a super and supportive mother, she was the recipient of many awards and honors as an educator and humanitarian.

ALISON TOWNSEND is a poet and essayist whose work has appeared in *The Georgia Review, Prairie, Schooner, Sing Heavenly Muse*, and *The Women's Review of Books*. She has been anthologized in *Poetry Loves Poetry* (Momentum, 1985) *Women and Stepfamilies: Voices of Anger and Love* (Temple, 1989) *And A Deer's Ear, Eagle's Song and Bear's Grace: Animals and Women* (Cleis, 1990) and *Woman Poet: The West II* (Women-In-Literature, 1991), held residences at

Dorland Mountain Colony and Cottages at Hedgebrook, and is a Lecturer in English at the University of Wisconsin-Platteville.

MARY DOAK TOWNSEND was born in 1919 in Philadelphia, Pennsylvania. She attended Smith College and the University of Pennsylvania, graduating with a degree in zoology, and worked for the American Friends Field Service before marrying Henry Townsend in 1947. They had three children and lived at Wild Run Farm in Pennsburg, Pennsylvania. Musically and artistically gifted, Mary is perhaps best described as a life enhancer whose tenderness, humor and affection touched everyone she met. She died of breast cancer in 1962.

LU VICKERS has had stories and poems published in *Common Lives, Calypso, Apalachee Quarterly* and *North of Wakulla, An Anhinga Anthology*. She teaches writing at Tallahassee Community College.

ALYCE ANNE VICKERS COLSON was born in Lakeland, Florida in 1932. She said she was crowned Homecoming Queen in 1950, but she could never find the photographs to prove it. She died in 1981.

HELEN VOZENILEK has written for and edited a number of publications. *Loss of the Ground-Note* is the first project of this scope she has taken on. She may or may not attempt something similar again. For gainful employment, she works as an electrician in the Bay Area. Putting this anthology together has been difficult and extremely rewarding. Maybe a little like motherhood.

MIROSLAVA SMRČKOVA was born in Czechoslovakia in 1921. She escaped from that country in 1948 and came to the United States shortly afterwards. She worked as a radiologist in Washington state for nearly thirty years. She loved to travel, play tennis and bridge and entertain. Miroslava was strong, independent and raised two children as a single mother. She died of cancer one week after her sixty-fifth birthday.

CAROLYN WEATHERS left her native Texas in 1968 to move to hippie Los Angeles, where she lives with her partner, artist Jenny Wrenn, and their three dogs. She is co-editor, with Wrenn, of *In A Different Light: An Anthology of Lesbian Writers* (Clothespin

Fever Press), a finalist for the American Library Association's Gay and Lesbian Book Award 1990. She has published three books (Clothespin Fever): *Leaving Texas: A Memoir, Shitkickers and Other Texas Stories* and *Crazy*. Her latest work is in *The Lone Star Literary Quarterly*, in*Common Bonds: Stories by and about Modern Texas Women* (Southern Methodist University Press) and *The Poetry of Lesbian Sex* (Banned Books). She and Wrenn run Clothespin Fever Press.

ALIDA NABORS WEATHERS HAYEN was the child of loving, hardworking Texas tenant farmers and worked as a domestic cook to save money for college. She dropped out of Baylor University in 1932 to marry ministry student Jones Weathers and returned twenty-six years later for her degree. Sweet, gentle, maternal, open-minded, intelligent, informed and plucky, she touched everyone who knew her with her kindness, graciousness and non-judgmental attitude. She died in 1988, more hopeful agnostic than Baptist believer, one day before her seventy-ninth birthday.

MARY JANE WESTBROOK studied art at Parsons School of Design and The New School for Social Research in New York City. She has recently earned an M.F.A. in sculpture from the California College of Arts and Crafts in Oakland. Currently, she is doing installations which involve text and light as sculptural elements. She lives in Oakland, California with her three cats Annie, Nou Nouch and Wolfman Jack.

JANE BASKIN WESTBROOK was a homemaker and served as both elder and deacon in the First Presbyterian Church in Bartlesville, Oklahoma. She also sang in the church choir and was a member of the Bell Choir. She played the piano, the trumpet and the violin. She tap danced and ate potato chips and drugstore sandwiches (not at the same time). She liked Bobby Darin, the Hallelujah Chorus and Hershey's Kisses. In her lifetime she had seventeen dogs and a horse named Flash. She died of ovarian cancer on June 12, 1988 at the age of sixty-seven.

JOANNA H. WOŚ is the youngest daughter of Polish parents who emigrated to the U.S. following World War II. She is also the mother of a five year old son and is married to a member of the Onondaga Indian Nation. She has worked in museums for sixteen years, most recently worked for the New York State Writers Institute, and has just moved to Santa Fe.

MARIA DZIĘGALA WOS´ was a Polish peasant who, in 1939, was taken from her home, along with her husband and two baby daughters, to a Soviet slave labor camp where her younger child died of starvation. After World War II, following the birth of two more daughters, one in England and one in the U.S., she died at the age of forty-six.

Are You Girls Traveling Alone?
Adventures in Lesbianic Logic by Marilyn Murphy
A selection of her columns that appeared in the Lesbian News, a
newsmagazine out of Los Angeles. Her feminism was lauded by
Gloria Steinem in her book *Revolution from Within*.
ISBN: 1-878533-03-7 $10.95

Crazy by Carolyn Weathers
This novel is a compassionate, hard-hitting account of a manic-depres-
sive breakdown and recovery. A high-wire balance act of gravity and
wit.   ISBN:0-9616572-3-5 $8.95

Dark Passages by Elizabeth Hall
A beautifully designed poetry chapbook of a lesbian writing about her
grief over the death of her lover. Presents an exquisite portrait of grief
and love. ISBN:0-9616572-8-6 $5.95

A Dyke's Bike Repair Handbook by Jill Taylor
Widely-reviewed how-to-repair your motorcycle book is sensible,
clearly illustrated and helpful to any bike lover.
ISBN:0-9616572-4-3 $8.95

Getting Away With Murder by Pele Plante
Hunters do it every season according to some. But CC, a semi-retired
therapist, was convinced that not just the deer were the victims but
wealthy widows were as well. Great crime suspense as CC and her
partner Barbara delve, often unasked and sometimes to a fault, into
other people's problems.   ISBN: 1-878533-00-2 $9.95

Guide to Women Book Publishers in the US for 1992/93
Lists publishing houses owned by women, types of books published,
from the one-woman publisher of gardening books to the largest
presses. ISBN: 0-9616572-7-8 $15.95

In A Different Light: an anthology of Lesbian writers
edited by Weathers and Wrenn
An American Library Award Finalist, the anthology of 29 writers
celebrates ececticism in short stories, poems and novel excerpts.
ISBN: 0-9616572-5-1 $9.95

Portraits: Sapphic Zest for Life
by Teresita Bosch
Exquisite poems that capture the essence of different characters
– a treasury of remembrance
ISBN: 1-878533-02-9 $7.95

Shitkickers & Other Texas Stories by Carolyn Weathers
A poignant but delightfully funny romp through Texas Stomps, tent
revivals and pre-Stonewall gay bars, with a rollicking comparative
tour of Texas and Los Angeles country-western bars. ISBN: 0-9616572-
6-X $7.95

Stories of a Homeland and Other Poems by Louise Moore
L.A. poet, Louise Moore shares her homeland stories of Knoxville,
Tennessee. No ISBN $6.95

Send your name and address to be on our mailing list and receive our
LesbianLine catalog & newsletter. Include $2.00 in stamps.

Clothespin Fever Press
5529 N. Figueroa St.
Los Angeles, CA 90042

Ask for our catalog of Women's History Post Cards